A Players Program

The Playbook For Building and Maintaining
Positive Team Culture and Relationships

By
Coach Jeff Howell

A Players Program

Program

The Playbook For Building and Maintaining
Positive Team Culture and Relationships

Table of Contents

○ Acknowledgments...1

○ Preface 6

○ My Why 9

○ Transition to Madison Christian School (MCS)............13

○ Madison Christian School Assistant Coaching Years .....16 .

○ Evolution from Assistant to Head Coach 19

○ 2013 Summer Practices Leading into First Season.........22

○ A Players Program 26

○ Stephanie Marie Howell.....................................35

○ Player/Parent Relationship 38

○ Athletic Director Relationship: "The Blueprint" 48

○ The Assistant Coach Dynamic.....................................53

○ Lady Eagles Program Development..............................57

○ Coach Howell's Skills and Drills Basketball Camp 60

○ Fellowship Activities 63

○ Ohio State Lady Buckeye Games 67

○ Service Projects and Partnerships 69

❍ It Takes a Village 74

❍ The Seasons 77

❍ Captains 89

❍ Wednesday Juice 91

❍ Senior Night: February 3, 2018 94

❍ The End of an Era 99

❍ The Final Season: 2022-23 102

❍ The Past: Lady Eagle Alumni 109

❍ Being a Great Teammate 111

❍ My Key Components To Program Success 121

❍ I Am Grateful … 128

Acknowledgments

J ust as it takes a village to maneuver a basketball program through the growth and maturation process, an amazing village has helped me in my coaching career, as well as crossing the finish line with this book.

First and foremost, I thank God for placing me in the right situation, at the right place, surrounded by the right people, at the right time. I have much work to do as I find my way with growth in my faith, but I have learned and discovered things within me that I did not even know I was capable of.

To Andy Scholz, my first and only Athletic Director for whom I ever worked, there are not enough words to describe how appreciative I am just for you giving me a chance to be your Head Girls' Basketball Coach. Thank you!

To Carole Witosky, Wendy Souzis, John Hamilton, and Camryn Howell, you rock in the athletic department. Thank you for your support!

Thank you to the Madison Christian School administration and staff for being supportive of me and my vision.

To Coach Mike Crabtree, you and your family have blessed me beyond measure. You are like a brother to me. I am so grateful to have worked by your side as we built the Lady Eagle program together.

To Coach Mike Kimbler, Coach Corey Payne, and Coach Tanner Grant, we have had many "fireside chats" talking about basketball and life, and I have learned so much from you over the years. However, the biggest value that you have given to me is just listening and being a sounding board for whatever I was going through. Thank you!

To Tay, Syd, and Cam, you were and continue to be my inspiration. I began the coaching journey because of you and the lack of girl-specific athletic opportunities when you were growing up. The three of you are simply amazing young ladies, and my love for you is infinite!

To Steph, my wife and the love of my life, you have always had my back and have been so supportive of any crazy ideas that I have had. You listen, you offer your thoughts and opinions, and most of all, you offer wisdom. You challenge me to seek answers from God in all that I do. I love you so much, and I am thankful to be your partner for 34 years.

To Tanya McClure-Harris, you are a role model to so many. Your faith-driven journey from High

School Basketball All American, Ohio State Lady Buckeye, wife, and mother has been an inspiration. The way you have fought challenges, adversity, and the few setbacks that have come your way gives me strength, and quite frankly, it gives me the energy to never give up. Your presence, consultative conversations, and on-court team training to improve the skill set of the girls were huge for the program, and I am forever thankful for you!

To every single student-athlete who has flowed through the Lady Eagle Basketball program, you are why there is "A Players Program", and you are what motivated me to continue this journey for nine years. I thank you for your patience, understanding, effort, hard work, and (most of all) your love. You made the experience so much fun, and you are directly responsible for my personal growth, which I will never, ever forget. I love you all so much!

Thank you, Lady Eagles' parents, for your unconditional support. You trusted me to do what I felt was best for the growth of your daughters, and you allowed me to push and challenge them to reach higher limits. I am so grateful for each of you.

To the Ohio High School Athletic Association (OHSAA), I thank you for allowing me to officiate in a first-class organization for 19 years. As a coach, I "only" received five technical fouls in my nine-year career, when my energy and passion should have earned me more. I am thankful for the relationship that I earned with the officiating fraternity, which perhaps saved me from getting more technical fouls. You are a great organization with many quality officials.

Thank you, Kimani Haley and KNotED by Kimani, for your editing prowess and for providing the direction that I needed to move this book project forward!

There are more folks to thank who have supported me in so many ways and who have crossed my path. If I missed your name, please accept my sincerest apologies, but know that I am thankful for you.

To my parents and family, Jason Hovance, Danielle Fleming, D'wan Vickroy, MOCAL Coaches, Brock Yutzy, Madison Christian Cheerleaders, Mandy Wray, Chris Bond, Ohio Health, Jenalle Crabtree, Amy Scholz, Jamal Luke, Dale Tucker Sr., Jill Woerner, Dr. Tim Houston, NABC Coaches Clinics, Ohio High School District 10, Hudl, Durand Sweatt, Lexi Doddridge, Tabby Hahn, Flyers's Pizza, Olive Branch Pizza, Janelle Maur, Erin Higginbotham Neal, Abigail Zwelling David, Patriot Preparatory Academy, Madison Christian Church, City of Obetz, City of Groveport, Craig Ross, 3Dimensional Coaching, Hoops 4 Christ, Girls Basketball Academy, Athletic Trainer Mike Eddington, Athletic Trainer Amanda Sampsel, Madison Christian Coaches, Smoothie King-Pickerington, The Baise Family, Tia Lamar, Lee Brockett, Sam Krafty, Bill Andrews, Lenny Powell,

Acknowledgments

Todd Starkey, Teresa Woerner, DJ Sharp, Todd Ska-hill, John Lidonnice, Jerome Ross, Turea Moore, Kevin Andewiel, Dr. Janell Jones, Kevin Fessenmeyer, Proforma Strategic Promotions.

Preface

"Working hard is one thing, but working hard with purpose is what separates the good from the great."
– Thad Matta

Every season started with a parent meeting and this was my written introduction to them.

Dear Parents:

My name is Jeff Howell, and I am very blessed to have the opportunity to coach your daughter in the game of basketball and to promote her growth on the court and off the court as well. My objective is to develop her basketball skills from the very fundamental aspects and add elements to her game in such a way that even she may not have known was within her. In addition, I am led to provide leadership skills, to function as a mentor or extension of your family unit, to maintain the mission of Madison Christian School, and to adhere to a God-first environment.

Some background about me:

- Certified Ohio High School Basketball Official for 19 years
- Two-year Varsity Assistant at the former Liberty Christian School (now Patriot Preparatory Academy)
- Varsity Assistant at Madison Christian
- Nine-year Head Coach at Madison Christian
- Husband for 34 years to my wife, Stephanie
- Father to three children: Tatum, Sydney, and Camryn
- Bachelor's degree in Business Administration from Ohio Dominican University
- Master's degree in Business Administration Leadership from Ohio Dominican University
- Director of National Sales with Cascade365 Liquidity Solutions
- Avid OSU Football and Basketball fan; 20-year OSU Lady Buckeye basketball season ticket holder
- Lifelong Pittsburgh Steeler fan (even though I grew up near Cincinnati, Ohio)

Two Fun Facts:

- *21-year Commissioner of a 12-team fantasy football league*
- *Recipient of the Home Economic - Student of the Year Award (as a senior in high school)*

  ○ *Why? I made the best Rice Krispy Treats!!!*

I thank you for your support, your prayers, and your patience. I promise, to the best of my ability, to have an influence on your daughter's life and to ensure that her basketball experience will be as memorable and rewarding for her as I know it will be for me.

**Source: Intro Section of the
Lady Eagle Parent Handbook**

My Why

"If you cannot figure out your purpose, figure out your passion. For your passion will lead you right into your purpose."
– Bishop T.D. Jakes

Throughout my lifetime, I have learned to live by these three rules:

1. If you do not go after what you want, you will never have it.
2. If you do not ask, the answer will always be "no".
3. If you do not step forward, you will always remain in the same place.

Raising three girls, I was the consummate "Girl Dad". I was involved in everything they chose to experience, be it sports, church, or school activities. My wife and I had a good balance that fit each of our personalities and styles. She brought the craft aspect, the ability to fix household items (which I cannot), and (most of all) the reminder that God was to be first in all that we sought. She was always looking for opportunities within the church that were age-specific for the girls to not only keep them involved but also to fellowship and make sure that they had growth from Christian experiences. For me, I brought structure, organization, time management, initiative-taking thought processes, and finally, the sports aspect. There is no doubt that I was joined at the hip with my wife as we raised our children, and the result has been three successful, intelligent, beautiful girls. I am thankful for my wife and my girls, and I love them with all my heart.

We got the girls involved in many sports when they were little: T-ball, soccer, karate, cheerleading (yes, it's a sport), and basketball. They were also active in many leadership activities through Triedstone Missionary Baptist Church, Delta Sigma Theta Sorority, Inc., *The Columbus Dispatch*, Junior Achievement, the Columbus Urban League, and the Blue-Chip Foundation. My thought process was that if you are not going to be successful in a sport, you are for sure going to be a leader and position yourself to set the foundation for future jobs and advancement. When the kids were growing up, team sports, such as basketball and soccer, were co-ed, and because the boys were more athletic, they played the game amongst themselves and rarely passed or shared the ball with a girl, forfeiting any opportunity to give the girl players any type of chance to see some success or gain confidence. Therefore, my girls just ran around getting their cardio workout without touching the ball or developing any skills in the sport. They were fine from a mindset perspective because (to them) running around and looking "sweet" in their uniforms and new shoes was cool. For me, it was frustrating, and unbeknownst to me at the time, it was also the foundational seed of what was to come.

I never thought of being a head basketball coach nor did I set my sights on that role. I began the coaching journey just out of a desire to hang out with my daughter during her high school years by being an assistant and offering value, perspective, and insight to the Head Coach from my experiences as an Ohio High School Basketball Official. Never in my wildest dreams would I have expected a nine-year coaching run nor the impact that I seemed to have on the students, their parents, their families, and the school administration.

The extent of my basketball experience included playing in high school at Delaware Hayes, being a 19-year OHSAA basketball official, and having a two-year stint as Assistant Basketball Coach at Liberty Christian Academy (now Patriot Preparatory Academy). The Liberty Christian years coincided with my older daughter's seasons as a basketball player and captain. The plan with her was the same as I had with my youngest daughter: cherish time with her, assist the head coach with his needs, and help mentor student-athletes. They were fun times for sure, but I was still in referee mode when it came to idle time away from my day job and I officiated as many games as I could. It was not until the transition to Madison Christian School that things began to change and officiating took a back seat.

Transition to Madison Christian School (MCS)

"If your actions inspire others to dream more, learn more, do more and become more, you are a leader."

– John Quincy Adams

We transitioned to MCS after Camryn's 7th-grade year at Patriot Preparatory Academy. We thought that entering as an eighth grader was a good transitional period because that is the year the school starts preparing them for the high school and college preparatory curriculum. She went through tryouts and was successful in making the junior high school basketball team. I watched from the stands during home and away games and supported her, the coach, and the team in any way that I could, which (most of the time) was simply with encouraging words and occasionally a rule interpretation for the coach.

During the middle of the season, I became "score-book guy" and sat at the courtside table during each game. I will admit that this became a problem because I had issues keeping my mouth shut and was essentially offering instruction and cheering on the girls, as well as sharing critical remarks to the officials in a fun way. I either knew or had officiated with most of the officials at some point, so that saved me from being removed from the scorer's table. However, the junior high head coach and I had a discussion, although it was more of him doing the talking, and I was advised to tone things down and let him coach. Message heard!!

After I was "scolded" in a Christian manner by the junior high head coach, I felt that perhaps, when my daughter transitioned to high school, I could be a better fit as an assistant coach at that level. I envisioned myself talking to the players, encouraging and cheering for them, offering constructive advice during games, speaking to the officials (in a respectful manner, of course), and most of all, doing this without the head coach getting upset with me and essentially telling me to stay in my lane. The Madison Christian High School Girls' Basketball head coach, at the time, was also a certified fitness trainer, and he offered to take my daughter under his wing for the summer with basketball-specific training and conditioning, as well as speed and agility improvement, twice a week. Not only was this a godsend for my daughter because she really thrived and seemed to enjoy this type of training because she could see the results, but I also developed a relationship with the head coach. I eventually was offered and accepted the invitation to be his assistant coach at Madison Christian School.

Madison Christian School Assistant Coaching Years

"Be more concerned with your character than your reputation, because your character is what you really are, while your reputation is merely what others think you are."

– John Wooden

The head coach came from a big school in Northwest Ohio where winning, in general, and winning state championships in multiple sports was the norm. He was not a parent to an MCS student and he was not a teacher or aide at MCS. He had never coached at MCS; therefore, he did not have a complete understanding of the MCS culture, the student demographic, and the overall mindset of the parents and school administration. His mindset from the jump was "We are here to win a state championship", and this was communicated regularly during practices. This is a very aspiring goal, and we all would certainly love to be a state champion; however, that is not where this team was or is to this day.

For a school like Madison Christian, where most of the athletes play multiple sports and do not put in the extra work required in the offseason to be state championship-ready, winning a district championship would be equivalent to winning a state championship for a small school such as ours. I noticed that his approach was not relationship-driven and came across as controlling with minimal input from the players or even me as his assistant. He was a nice guy with really promising ideas, solid practice plans, and certainly the knowledge of what it takes to be a champion. However, what he underestimated was the talent level and commitment of the girls to want to put in the necessary work to develop a championship pedigree. I learned, during his tenure, that it was important to get to know and understand the girls, regarding what they want to accomplish on the court, off the court, and in life, and to earn their respect and the respect of their parents.

In reflection, these are really the core ingredients to being a successful head coach, and all equate to building a relationship. Because of the time I spent in getting to know most of the girls and their parents during their junior high school years and, of course, with my tie to the school as a parent, I became the sounding board for many complaints that the team had toward the head coach. I was the energy guy and always the first to compliment on a good play and encourage on a bad play. I listened to them and communicated my thoughts on how to manage the adversity that they were dealing with at the time. I gained their trust because I was a part of the MCS family. I took a vastly different approach than the head coach, as the assistant, so this made things a bit easier and less confrontational to the team. Unbeknownst to me at the time, the seeds were planted for what was about to happen soon.

Evolution from Assistant to Head Coach

"God has planted greatness in you. Let today be the beginning of a great adventure as you step into the gifts He has given you."
— Joyce Meyer

There was a lot of tension during my time as the assistant coach for the Lady Eagles. Many of the girls, frankly, did not like the head coach; the head coach was not willing to accept suggestions related to game management from me, and tension was mounting between the head coach and the athletic director, who sometimes would offer constructive thoughts related to the team that were brushed aside by the head coach. I do not know if these factors set him up for failure, but it is hard to imagine these things not contributing to what was about to happen next.

Madison Christian School is a private Christian school located in Groveport, Ohio, a suburb of Columbus, Ohio, and has served the community for over 40 years. The mission of MCS is to partner with parents and churches to lead students toward God, while scripturally educating the whole person - spiritually, academically, emotionally, socially, and physically - to become strong Christian leaders. Madison Christian School exists to glorify God and to promote the following core values: Prayer, Love, Unity, God's Word, Family-Centered Focus, Evangelism and Discipleship, Excellence, and Service (**Source: MCS Website**). I provide this background about the school because (regardless of whether it is fair or unfair) there are different standards in play at Madison Christian School compared to a public school or any school with a non-Christian component. As a stakeholder of the school (whether you are an administrator, teacher, coach, parent, or student), it is important that your choices are consistent inside and outside of Madison Christian School.

During the Spring of 2013, the head coach made some inappropriate decisions that were posted on social media; these decisions were not in alignment with being a leader of a Christian school (nor any school where you are charged with being a role model and mentor to students). I received a call from the athletic director in May 2013 (less than one month from when OHSAA allows for summer team basketball practices to begin) asking if I wanted to be the interim head coach during summer conditioning and practices with the long-term plan of me becoming the head coach when we got closer to the winter basketball season and upon school board approval. WOW!!! Obviously, the athletic director was in a tough position since summer practices were to begin in a few short weeks, and going through the process of finding a new Head Coach at this point in the year when most coaching vacancies were filled would be difficult. Therefore, a guy, who has no head coaching experience, has now been thrust into the position of being the leader of an Ohio high school girls basketball team.

Before I conclude this chapter, I want to acknowledge the head coach, whom I assisted at Madison Christian School. He was a thoughtful person and had good intentions for the kids. He was motivated to make them better on the court and really wanted to change the program into a championship culture. He helped my daughter by motivating her to be a well-conditioned person, whether she planned to pursue sports at the next level or not, and for that, I will always be appreciative. He was instrumental in my growth, spiritually, and taught me to be comfortable with praying aloud in front of the team and groups. He has since passed away, but he will forever have a place in my heart; I am grateful that he came into the lives of my family and me.

2013 Summer Practices Leading into First Season

"Thankfulness is the beginning of gratitude.
Gratitude is the completion of thankfulness.
Thankfulness may consist merely of words.
Gratitude is shown in acts."
– Henri Frederic Amiel

The summer basketball season is ten days of coach-led team practices, which the Ohio High School Athletic Association (OHSAA) allows in the month of June. These practices can be scrimmages against other teams or regular practices where they focus on conditioning, fundamentals, or offense/ defense implementation. We rarely had more than five players at any of the summer practices. Vacations, other sports priorities, or just kids having no interest in working out and getting better were typically the themes. Thus, all we could do was condition, work on fundamentals through miscellaneous drills related to ball handling, shooting, and passing, and play 2-on-2 or 3-on-3 competition. Because I only had a few weeks to prepare for summer practices and no assistant coach at the time, I utilized Google or You-Tube to find appropriate basketball drills that were easy enough for the girls to understand while (at the same time) hoping that it would help improve their overall skill set.

When summer practices concluded around the third week of June, I went to work on getting ready for the upcoming season, assuming that I was going to officially be named the head coach sometime in the coming weeks. I attended two coaching clinics, one in Nashville, Tennessee and one in Columbus, Ohio, to listen to some of the best coaches in the country share their coaching philosophy, offensive and defensive techniques, full and half court pressure, how to break presses, out of bounds plays, and so much more. It was a lot, but I became a sponge. However, much of what I learned was about team identity and cultures that they created within their programs and the importance of laying this foundation early and often to set up the team for success. Outside of these coaching clinics, I also leaned on many coaching friends, whom I met while officiating their games, to gain direction, advice, and confidence. I prayed for clarity to pull it all together so that when I communicated to the team, they would have a clear understanding of what I was trying to translate to them.

Around September 2013, my athletic director made it official that I would be named "Head Coach" of the Madison Christian Lady Eagle Basketball team. There were emotions of excitement, anxiety, and nervousness throughout me when I was informed. There was so much to do to prepare and so many components to integrate when I had to remind myself that I had a full-time day job! Before I could get into the X's and O's of what we wanted to accomplish on the court and how, I had to tackle the culture and mindset of the program and create an identity of who we were and who we wanted to be. The current mindset of many of the girls was to play a winter sport so that they did not have to take a gym class.

Consequently, several of the girls were playing a sport that they could care less about playing, were not willing to put in the extra work needed to get better, and essentially were only going through the motions of being a basketball player. In most large programs, they would have been cut from the team, but because the numbers of the girl's program were so low at the time, we needed bodies to fill a team. Short-term, I had to try and bring a spark back to the current team and their parents because of many tough and losing seasons, but long term, I knew that I would need to bring enthusiasm to the entire program to get students excited to come out and play basketball. I needed to promote my vision for the future and create a program that was inclusive, competitive, and most of all fun. It would be a difficult and time-consuming task, but I had a plan.

A Players Program

"And whether one member suffer, all the
members suffer with it; or if one member is
honored, all the members rejoice with it."
– 1 Corinthians 12:26

There have been two key areas that have helped
me in life: playing team sports while growing up
and having a successful career in sales. Team sports
helped me to learn about trust, compromise, working
in groups, accountability, responsibility, work effort,
goals, and so much more. Sales has helped my growth
in relation to dealing with people and differing personalities, having a vision, being strategic, handling
objections, cultivating relationships, being organized
and structured, and so much more. These elements
are on full display when coaching a team. My vision
was to create an identity that was simple to understand and something that the girls could easily share

with others inside and outside of the basketball program. The identity had to be something in which we all believed, and eventually, I was confident that this team identity would lead to the culture change that I wanted for this basketball program.

I had heard the phrase "A Players Program" from two prominent NCAA D1 women's basketball teams in the past. What I did not know was what the phrase was interpreted to mean or the components of this phrase for their programs. Through many discussions with my athletic director related to goals, objectives, climate of the school, and athletics, in general, it became clear what I wanted the vision and identity of the program to be. I took "A Players Program" to new levels within Lady Eagles Basketball and added detailed context, scripture, and five components with definitions for each. I then approached my pastor at Triedstone Missionary Baptist Church to explain the vision to him and sought guidance with biblical references to associate with each component. Below is the meaning of "A Players Program" and the identity of the Lady Eagles Basketball Program.

—

Lady Eagle Varsity Basketball of Madison Christian School has an identity that embraces the core goals, values, and objectives of the program.

A Players Program consists of five unique components:

1. **God First and Service**
2. **Past**
3. **Present**
4. **Future**
5. **JUICE!**

God First and Service

Romans 12:1

I beseech you therefore, brethren, by the mercies of God, that ye present your bodies a living sacrifice, holy, acceptable unto God, which is your reasonable service.

- King James Version

Everything that we, as coaches and as players, do on and off the court will be in honor of and to honor God's grace.

- Players and coaches will keep God foremost in our minds during interactions with other players, coaches, teammates, officials, administrators, teachers, parents, family members, and friends.
- We all will serve God to the best of our abilities and take a lead-by-example approach in everything that we do.

- We will service the community in a fashion that assists those who are less fortunate than ourselves.
- We will partner with The Bridgeway Academy Therapy Center of Columbus, Ohio. Eagles for a Cause is in place to provide service and donations to children with special needs and to those who are less fortunate than we are.

Past

Matthew 5:16

Let your light so shine before men, that they may see your good works, and glorify your Father which is in heaven.

- We welcome former Lady Eagle basketball players to continue to be a part of the program.
- We want our Lady Eagle basketball alumni to come "home" to fellowship with current team members and coaches, to participate in practices, pray with us, to lead devotions, to participate in "All-In" athletic activities, and to remain engaged with the program.
- Past MCS Lady Eagle basketball players are important to the present team members in that they have been through the rigors of being a student-athlete, and they can be excellent mentors.

- The former captain(s) from the prior season have agreed to write a letter to future captains, only to be opened upon their selection in the new season. The letter will emphasize the suggested characteristics, responsibilities, accountabilities, and leadership necessary to be an MCS Lady Eagle Captain. This document will be the blueprint to follow for the future captains.
- We plan to have alumni games where past Lady Eagles will play present Lady Eagles.
- The Past is always welcome in the Present as well as the Future.

Present

Proverbs 22:6

Train up a child in the way he should go and when he is old, he will not depart from it.

- Our current players are the face of the Lady Eagle Basketball Program.
- As coaches, we are charged with developing players on and off the court. We want to develop, improve, and maintain their basketball skills while, at the same time, facilitate their growth into leaders and prepare them for life challenges ahead.
- As coaches, we are not a parent to our players nor a parental replacement; however, our role

is to complement the parent and assist the student-athletes as they move to the next level of experiences that they will encounter.

- We want to engage our parents to become involved and support the program as best as they can, and we certainly encourage an open-door policy to constructively discuss the progress of their student-athletes.
- We will engage in off-court activities such as Lady Buckeye basketball games, meals, service projects, speakers, and many more fellowship activities.

Future

Romans 15:1-2

We then that are strong ought to bear the infirmities of the weak, and not to please ourselves. Let every one of us please his neighbor for his good to edification.

- The future is our junior high girls basketball program.
- High school players and the coaching staff are charged with being mentors to the girls at the junior high level. In addition, we will be role models to the best of our ability and will take a lead-by-example approach with them.

- Each summer, we will conduct multiple girls' basketball camps for girls entering third through eighth grades. These camps will prepare them for the court, offer off-the-court life lessons, and allow them to share Christian experiences.
- The coaching staff and team members will be fully active with the MCYAL (Madison Christian Youth Athletic League) youth program at Madison Christian School and will assist in drill and skill sessions, games and offer direction as needed.
- We will assist the junior high school basketball program in any way that we can, work hand-in-hand with the coaching staff, and help when needed or called upon.
- We will fully support the junior high school basketball program at their games whenever possible.
- We want to prepare the eighth graders for the high school level as far as expectations and challenges ahead so that they hit the ground running. Our senior leadership will also speak to the junior high school team to offer guidance as they prepare to enter high school.

JUICE!

Isaiah 40:29

He gives strength to the weary and increases the power of the weak

Psalm 119:114

You are my refuge and my shield; I have put my hope in your word.

- When we break a huddle we say, "Juice"; when we start practice, we say, "Juice"; when we end practice we say, "Juice"; before the game, we say, "Juice"; during the game, we want to "Bring the Juice!"
- "Juice" means many things to the Lady Eagle Basketball Program.

  - For example, Trust in God, Energy, Believe, Optimism, Offense, Defense, Push Forward, Encourage, Fight Through Adversity, Strength, Success, Motivation and more

- Juice represents a value that comes from within that will carry you as an individual and the team to the positive results that are desired.

With the identity established and in writing for reference, our actions needed to be consistent to establish the culture that I wanted for this team. To promote "A Players Program", I created a specific Lady Eagles Coach social media account on Instagram and Facebook, provided handouts of our identity at parent meetings, discussed "A Players Program" with the junior high school girls' coach and team, and shared our identity with Madison Christian School staff and stakeholders. Everyone knew that change was in the air, and a cultural shift was occurring. My approach was in the process of taking off, and I was prepared for the transition and the highs and lows that came with it.

The first year was tough because everything was so new, and the student-athletes were not accustomed to the philosophical approach that I was taking with the team. However, summer participation was up in year 2, and by the third summer, numbers consistently reached double digits every year. We were now ready to thrive in our new identity of "A Players Program" and what would become the established culture of the Lady Eagle program going forward.

Stephanie Marie Howell

"People will forget what you said, people will forget what you did, but people will never forget how you made them feel"
— Maya Angelou

This is a good spot to mention my wife (of 34 years at the time of this writing). For me, I immersed myself in all aspects of coaching with the goal of putting in the time required to do it the right way. My way may not be the right way for all coaches, but I did not have a blueprint to follow. Therefore, I took what I felt to be a commonsense approach to being a head coach. A coach at a higher-level school with different dynamics related to competitiveness, pressures to win, culture, academics, etc., may have a much different game plan for coaching than I do. However, in the end, my approach was the right fit for the girls at Madison Christian School.

My approach encompassed maximum allowable hours of practice time, game days, film study, scouting, applicable and relevant individual and team meetings before or after practice, captains' meetings, coaches' meetings, athletic director meetings, parent meetings, service projects on weekends, attending junior high school basketball games, volunteering four hours at MCS youth basketball clinics on Saturdays, attending non-basketball activities of players, and much more. I was consumed with growing and maintaining youth/player/parent relationships regardless of day or time. All these actions took time and time away from my home and my wife.

I am more than thankful that Stephanie could see the passion that I had for wanting these kids to be successful and to grow and mature under my leadership. She could clearly see the results of these efforts, and she became my biggest cheerleader throughout my nine-year journey. She saw my joy when things were going well, and she felt my sorrow during times of adversity. She listened and gave me her perspective when a parent complained about issues related to their daughter or during miscellaneous tough decisions or moments. She offered advice after games on what she saw on the court, and she participated in off-court activities with me and the team and had fun interacting with everyone. Most of all, she let me do my thing for nine years with minimal complaints. She could see the positivity in what I was doing and how the girls seemed to look up to me as a role model and mentor. She could see the growth that they were experiencing through their time under my leadership. Not every coach's spouse can or will give in to the requirements of what a coach needs to do to be successful because it is a lot, and it is a sacrifice. I cannot say enough how much I love and respect my wife for allowing me the freedom to do what was necessary to have a successful basketball program, which also facilitated my growth as a person.

Player/Parent Relationship

"I can affect change by transforming the only thing that I ever had control over in the first place and that is myself."
— Deepak Chopra

My background in sales has helped me so much with creating and maintaining relationships, which in turn translates into long-term partnerships. I have taken the same approach with players and their parents. With the players, I wanted to understand what they liked or disliked on and off the court, what other school activities they were involved in, what they did off the court in their spare time, what their college options were, the major they wanted to focus on in college, and what career they wanted after college. We have done vision boards to help the girls think about their futures and to help me understand who they are and their mindsets. By understanding the players, I was able to help them progress toward achieving their future goals.

Player relationships, from my perspective, also included attending activities that did not necessarily involve basketball, in order to show my genuine interest in them and their growth. This was one of my favorite things to do. I have attended summer AAU basketball games, soccer, softball, and volleyball games for both high school and club, track & field events, choir and band concerts, violin performances, graduations, and much more. It is refreshing to see how talented these girls are and the hard work that they put forth on and off the basketball court.

Player Testimonial

The first thing that comes to mind when I think about Coach Howell is a father figure. He always showed his love for his players by attending events outside of the basketball realm. For me, these events included soccer games, track meets, and even academic events such as my National Honor Society ceremony and my graduation. It showed his dedication to not only supporting his players in athletics but also his confidence in his players' academic achievements. These extra efforts led to my developing a close relationship with Coach Howell which allowed me to treat the sport as something fun to fill my free time as opposed to another burden in my high school career. Anytime any of us needed anything, we were always comfortable asking him because we knew he would try to help us the best he could.

Most importantly, something I appreciated the most about Coach Howell is that we shared a genuine connection in keeping each other accountable. If players' academics were slipping, Coach would always know and try to help us improve. He gave us as players the opportunity to keep him accountable as well by always asking how he could improve his coaching methods, attitude, practice, and game plans to ensure that we were successful as a team. This informality in the relationship helped build the care and trust we still have today for one another on and off the court. I am so blessed to know that he'll always have my back no matter the circumstance.

Lady Eagle Player and Alumni

With parents, it starts with communication. Any communication that I had with a player related to updates, schedule changes, practice day/times, etc., I always copied and included the parent. My athletic director taught me to protect myself and the school by sharing with me that if I send a text or email message to a player, I need to always include the parent. Every Sunday during the season, players and parents would receive a text from me about the upcoming week's practice and/or game schedule as well as any other events that we may have planned for that week. Even though this information was typically on the school athletic calendar, I over-communicated to ensure that no one missed anything, especially if a last-minute change to the schedule occurred. I also made a point to speak with parents and to get to know them at any chance that I could before and after games and practices and during the boys' games. I wanted to be approachable, and I wanted parents to feel comfortable speaking with me about anything.

Our practices were open to any parent who wanted to attend. Although only a few took advantage of my offer over the years, I welcomed any parent to come to watch practice and see what we were doing to get better as a team and for their daughter individually. To me, getting to know parents on a personal level and giving them an open invitation to practice created easier conversations and shed light as to why their daughter may not be getting the playing time that they perceived her to deserve. Thankfully, in nine years of coaching, I only had one issue where a parent expressed concerns to me about their kid's playing time.

Below is the standard information that I included in the Parent Handbook that was provided at the beginning of each season.

Parent Expectations and Coach's Comment

Parents:

Thank you! I have been a parent to three student-athletes, and I understand the rigors of your time, transportation, stress, money invested, and just the general feeling of being tired. I appreciate your sacrifice, and I am thankful for all that you do to assist me in making this experience as enjoyable as possible.

I only have two expectations:

- **R. A. C. E.**
  - **RESPECT one another,**
  - **Have a good ATTITUDE,**
  - **Be COACHABLE, and**
  - **Give maximum EFFORT in practices, games, and the classroom**

- I expect you to talk to me at any time: day, night, in person, over the phone, via text, and/ or via email. I welcome feedback, and I welcome constructive criticism that may help improve our team and your child's experience. I am by no means perfect, nor do I have all the answers; however, I do seek God's guidance in every decision that I make, and I welcome your thoughts as well. I want to discuss any concerns with you and work together on ways to ensure success and positive outcomes for your daughter.

PLAYING TIME IS NOT PROMISED

- Playing time is earned in practice and is primarily based on effort, attitude, and the ability to help our team be successful. If you ever want to discuss any concerns related to playing time, I will meet with you and the student-athlete together so that we can have a constructive conversation with no misunderstandings.

Practice Expectations

- Players are expected to be ready for the reading and discussion of our scripture of the day at the required practice time. It is important to be at practice to understand all that we are doing on the court related to plays, offense, defense, etc.

Practice Attendance

- Players or parents must contact me or the Assistant Head Coach directly via phone/text if a practice/game will be missed.

  - There is no teammate-sharing/communicating that a player will be absent from practice/game.

- No warnings about this. Accountability / Responsibility / Safety Concern

- Missed Practice Day before a game.

  ○ **Miss one quarter of the next game**

- Missed practice day before a game AND no contact.

  ○ **Miss 1st half of the next game**

- Multiple missed practices (6+).

  ○ **Miss 1st half of the next game**

- Tardiness to practice unless excused (Conditioning).

Game Expectations

- Unless otherwise instructed, arrive to all home and away games at least 45 minutes before game time ready to play.
- Gray uniforms (Away) and White uniforms (Home).
- Transportation: No bus / need parent driver assistance.

Communication

- Every Sunday I will send the calendar for that week to players and parents. Yes, I over-communicate!
- If you have any questions or comments, please contact me directly via phone or text.

Practice Attire

When MCS students, parents, and guests are attending school-related activities, apparel must be modest, appropriate for our conservative Christian community, and God-honoring. We ask that you follow the specific guidelines below.

- Shirts
    - T-shirts may be sleeveless (not side-less)
    - No visible undergarments or skin
    - No skin should show around the waist when arms are raised.
    - Modest necklines
    - No tank tops

- Shorts/Pants
    - Shorts must be loose fitting (compression or lycra shorts underneath is fine)
    - No writing on the back side
    - Shorts modest in length
    - If leggings are worn, loose fitting shorts must be worn over them

Lady Eagle Parent Testimonial

My wife and I have had the pleasure of knowing Coach Jeff for the last four years, and he has shown himself to be a man of both integrity and honor toward parents, athletes, Madison Christian School, and the athletic staff.

During that time, Coach Jeff has shown our daughter and the other girls in his program what it meant to be a team (both on and off the court) by sharing time to help them improve on the court and by coordinating off court activities, such as going to OSU Women's Basketball games, organizing team building getaways, and so much more. Though our daughter had no previous experience playing basketball before her freshman year, she had the heart of an athlete and the desire to improve and be a part of a team. Coach Jeff recognized this, and even though our daughter did not make the team her freshman year, she became the Team Manager. Coach Jeff offered to train her with the team and also gave her personal on-court training during his free time. Because of Coach Jeff's efforts, our daughter's abilities and confidence grew each year to the point of her developing into a very fine basketball player with a desire to be a well-developed athlete. To us, this entire journey began with a man who looked outside of a sport and into the lives of young women. His passion along with Christian principles have contributed to Coach Jeff molding his teams into incredibly well rounded, mature, young ladies with leadership qualities that they will use for the rest of their lives.

Mr. & Mrs. Cannon
Lady Eagle Parents

Athletic Director Relationship: "The Blueprint"

"Arrogance requires advertising. Confidence speaks for itself."
– Mike Krzyzewski

I have only worked for one athletic director in my coaching career, and I am just going to put it out there that he was an incredible athletic director ... PERIOD!! He is the "Blueprint" for any current or aspiring high school athletic director to follow. He held this role for 23 years at Madison Christian School and has won multiple Ohio State Athletic Director of the Year Awards. From the outset, he and I were on the same page as far as the direction that we wanted for not only the high school team but also the overall girls' basketball program. Was winning important? Yes, we wanted to win; however, is it the principal component on which the coaching staff should be focused or graded on? No! What was important to the athletic director was in direct correlation with the Madison Christian School Athletic Mission Statement:

"Madison Christian School Athletics, in alignment with the school's mission, seeks to use the pursuit of athletic excellence to develop strong Christian leaders by investing in the growth of the student athlete's faith, character, and leadership."

We both had a clear understanding of the student dynamic that we had at Madison Christian School which correlated to the historical student work ethic related to athletics, and the fact that we did not have the numbers for an athlete to focus only on one sport. Kids come to Madison Christian School for structure, academics, and the Christian experience, not to propel them in a sport that will move them to the next level of athletics. It is an incredibly special time when we have students sign letters of intent to play a college sport after graduating from Madison Christian School because it does not happen consistently.

I knew that I had to be different if I wanted to change the culture, and I was very aware that to be different I needed to bring other elements to the high school basketball experience that did not involve passing, dribbling, and shooting a basketball. I shared with my athletic director my plans to bring outside help to the team, which would prepare the girls for life experiences, and I also shared my plans for miscellaneous service projects that would enlighten them and allow them to give back the blessing that was given to them. I shared my vision on camps, partnerships, raising dollars for the program, outside activities such as OSU Lady Buckeye Basketball games, etc., and he was on board with everything. If he did not like an idea, he would always have another way of accomplishing the same thing, just with a different approach.

Although he rarely said "no" to an idea that I had, when he did, I always respected his decision. What made him unique was that when "no" was the response to an idea or suggestion, he had a solution to offset the denial, which in the end made sense once explained. Our communication with each other was phenomenal, and I could share anything with him in strict confidence. Over time, I earned his trust where he could share sensitive things with me and be confident that what he shared would always stay with me and no one else. Our vision and plans for the Lady Eagle basketball program were proactive, efficient and in sync, and together we had a powerful nine-year run of on and off court success. We communicated often (regardless of the time of day/night), shared goals and objectives, and were honest and realistic with each other. I am thankful for my athletic director, his family, and the partnership that we had together. I can say without hesitation that not only was he an incredible boss, but he was and remains my friend.

Athletic Director Testimonial

Jeff has demonstrated an exceptional talent for not only coaching the technical aspects of the game but also for nurturing an environment where players feel supported, encouraged, and empowered. His emphasis on building and maintaining positive relationships within the team is truly commendable and has undoubtedly contributed to the success of the program.

The "A Players Program" that Jeff has implemented reflects his deep understanding of the importance of cultivating a culture of excellence. By emphasizing the development of not just skilled athletes but also well-rounded individuals who exhibit qualities of leadership, teamwork, and resilience, Jeff has created a framework that sets his players up for success both on and off the court.

Under Jeff's leadership, the girls' basketball program at Madison Christian School has flourished, not only in terms of wins and losses but also in the growth and personal development of the players. His commitment to instilling values of sportsmanship, integrity, and discipline is evident in the way his players carry themselves both during games and in their everyday lives.

I wholeheartedly endorse Jeff Howell and his coaching philosophy. His passion for the game, combined with his dedication to creating a positive and supportive team culture, make his insight an invaluable asset to any athletic program. I have no doubt that Jeff's experience and passion will continue to enhance his efforts in the realm of athletics moving forward.

Andy Scholz
Madison Christian Athletic Director
2000-2023

The Assistant Coach Dynamic

"A coach is someone who tells you what you don't want to hear, who has you see what you don't want to see so you can be who you've always known you could be."
– Tom Landry

During the first year (or should I say the transition year) when I was thrust into the head coaching position, I was honestly just looking for an assistant coach to be there to help with splitting up the team to do miscellaneous drills and to be another set of eyes on the court. I had zero expectations for an assistant coach … initially. A parent of one of the players volunteered to be my first-ever assistant coach, and he was dependable and offered good insight. The issue that came up periodically during the initial season was that he was a little tougher on his own kid, which at times caused some uncomfortable situations. I addressed it with him on several occasions, but it continued into year two. After consulting with the AD, I had to make a difficult decision to let him go after an early season scrimmage in the best interest of the team.

I was able to get an interim assistant who was also the junior high girls' coach at the time. He was able to join me when there was not a conflict of games, and I was extremely appreciative of him and his time. We clicked very well, and I learned from him. He was knowledgeable and supportive, and he possessed the many qualities that I felt a good assistant should have. Unfortunately, he had his sights set on coaching on the boys' side where he felt he could add more value, and I certainly respected and supported him in every way.

In year three of my coaching career, I found "My Guy". I had been "courting" him for a while, and the timing finally clicked as he transitioned from being the Madison Christian Boys' Head Coach, which also coincided with his daughter entering high school. I knew the high-quality coach that he was, but I did not have huge expectations of him other than being joined at the hip with me and helping to promote the vision that I had for the team, now and in the future. Having him by my side was a blessing because I was still new to coaching, and he had so much experience coaching the varsity boys. We clicked from the jump! He was a human "Google Search" of conditioning and basketball drills; he was very skilled from the offensive side of the ball with motion and plays. He was very easy to talk to and share things with, and we texted each other daily to discuss practice plans, game feedback, player performance, and the placement of the girls in the best possible situations to be successful.

We had disagreements at times, but this was good from my perspective. I never wanted my personality and approach to be controlling. I wanted to hear his ideas of the way we should do certain things; I wanted the pushback, and I needed it so that I could thoroughly look at the entire situation and make the best decisions for the team. I respected him, his knowledge, and his opinions, and I could feel that I earned his respect as well. He thoroughly understood the big picture and vision that I had for the Lady Eagles, and together we had a phenomenal seven-year run.

Over the years together, I never thought of him as my assistant coach. He had been a head coach for quite a few years, and I wanted him to be as comfortable as possible in the new role of assisting me. That is why I always referred to him as my "assistant head coach". Most of our decisions were made together, he typically led the start of practices with his drills or conditioning exercises, and he also was the lead in the offenses that we implemented and executed. I usually took the lead on the defensive schemes that we wanted to do throughout the season or for a specific game, as well as in game management. We had a clear understanding of each other's strengths; we communicated effectively, and we were in sync to proactively field competitive teams and achieve our goals and objectives. He is a great coach, faithful, dependable, and I am extremely grateful to call him and his family my friends.

Lady Eagles Program Development

"No matter how many mistakes you make or how slow the progress, you're still way ahead of everyone who isn't trying."
– Tony Robbins

When most consider sending their child to Madison Christian School, which is a private school, athletics is not at the top of the list of priorities. Christian focus, academics, structure, and overall values are typical priorities of parents when considering Madison Christian School, and these were the top priorities when we were looking for schools for our daughter. We knew nothing about the dynamics of their athletic programs other than the sports that were offered, and frankly, it did not matter. There are some private schools that make athletics a primary focus and consider academics and other key areas as lower priorities. These schools will "recruit" or highly influence student-athletes and their parents to make the switch to their school with the hope that this will create a winning program. This was not my approach, and I am thankful that it was not the approach or belief of my athletic director. We both had the belief that building from within, by developing our Kindergarten through sixth graders via the MCYAL (Madison Christian Youth Athletic League) program, was the pedestal to use for not only fundamental improvement but also student-athlete and parent relationship growth as well.

I was not the MCYAL lead as far as weekly agenda planning during the November through December time that MCYAL basketball ran, but I made sure that I was a presence every Saturday during the six-week period for basketball. I was regularly there at 10:00 AM for the Kindergarten through second-grade group, and I was finished at 2:00 PM by working with the third through sixth-grade groups. It is fulfilling to see how these kids really enjoy the personal attention they receive and how much just receiving a high five for making a good play or effort uplifts them. My objective was to show them how to get better and to be encouraging to them, even if mistakes were made. I also requested that members of our high school girls' basketball team volunteer their services to assist on these Saturdays as well. The presence we had by being around these kids uplifted them and all of us as well.

Being involved with MCYAL allowed me to meet many of the parents of the girls who participated. Introducing myself as the Madison Christian School High School Girls Basketball Coach was important, and it meant a lot to them that I was taking the time to help their daughters get better in the game of basketball. Since I began having yearly girls basketball camps, it also provided me with an avenue to share camp information and gather their contact information to communicate camp updates. However, the most positive aspect of my parent interaction was the formative beginnings of a relationship with parents as their children progressed toward high school.

Coach Howell's Skills and Drills Basketball Camp

*Never discourage anyone who continually
makes progress no matter how slow.*

– Pluto

*"Welcome them where they are and then
coach them toward who they can become."*

– Proactive Coaching

Although MCYAL was the foundation of my program building, my basketball camp became an important complimentary extension of their growth. The first year of my camp was the following summer at the end of my first year of coaching. I wanted something different than typical camps where all the kids do is learn fundamentals and play competitive games. I wanted to add a life and leadership component; I wanted speakers from churches, other coaches, sports figures, etc., to come speak to the girls on topics that related to their experiences, motivations, and other areas of growth. I also wanted former Lady Eagle alumni to participate and "give back" by discussing their basketball and academic experiences when they were sitting in the same seats in which the campers were currently sitting. The camps that I organized every June for nine years were incredibly successful and uplifting, and the girls left the camps not only with better basketball skills but also being extremely motivated.

The camps ran for two days (on a Friday and Saturday, typically around the third weekend of June). I had help from my assistant head coach, current and former Lady Eagle team members, the athletic director, the junior high school girls' basketball coach, the Madison Christian boys' coach, and many others from Madison Christian. We did many fundamental drills related to ball handling, shooting, and passing. We played competitive 3-on-3 and 5-on-5 basketball games and split teams based on skill level or grade. We also incorporated high school level fitness drills, which included speed and agility training, band usage, and low-level weightlifting with medicine balls. Through the years, I was able to bring two to three speakers to the camp every year, which included the pastor from my church, a former OSU Football National Champion from 2001, current and former OSU Lady Buckeye Basketball members, coaches, and the biggest hit, former Lady Eagle basketball players.

I called it "Alumni Roundtable", and every year, I would ask three former Lady Eagles to come to the camp and spend 20 minutes gathered around the campers at center court while I moderated with questions that were related to their academic and athletic journeys, challenges they faced, balancing schoolwork with athletic practices and games, adjusting from junior high to high school and high school to college, and many other questions. The alumni loved coming back to share their experiences, and the campers were eyes-wide-open and full of questions that would help them along their personal journeys. This yearly camp was special to me, and I always wanted to make sure that it was extra special and memorable to every camper who participated.

Fellowship Activities

"Champions are not made in gyms. Champions are made from something they have deep inside them – a desire, a dream, a vision. They must have the skill, and the will. But the will must be stronger than the skill."
– Muhammad Ali

Program building also encompassed off court activities and just spending time together as a team. Three important and critical areas for growth and relationship building are: 1) player learning about player; 2) player learning about coach; and 3) coach learning about player. It is amazing what you learn about a player during non-basketball-related activities, and I am sure that they learned a lot about me as well because of my transparency about my life experiences.

I was very intentional and planned fun, educational and service-related projects and activities off the court during the season and in the summer off-season. Projects in which we would fellowship or "give back" with time and service included attending Ohio State Lady Buckeye Basketball games, volunteering at an elementary school for their "Raising a Reader" literacy event, visiting an assisted living home and so much more. Over a nine-year period, our end of season fellowship included a lot of food and incorporated some fun activities, such as having a magician entertain us, Dave & Busters, an Escape Room (including the team and parents) and much more. We were the true essence of "Pray Hard, Play Hard, Stay Humble."

Our team put in the demanding work during the offseason, practices, and games; therefore, I wanted to reward them with fun and memorable activities throughout the season. It was my hope that they would cherish and look back upon these memories over a lifetime. I felt that playing high school basketball should be a high-level experience for all but especially for the seniors. When those girls became seniors, everyone (including the coaching staff) raised the bar a notch with urgency by doing all that we could to ensure not only a winning season but that they leave this program on a high note.

An exercise that was extremely popular with the girls and allowed us to learn about one another as far as what we want to do and where we want to be in our lives were Vision Boards. The intention of Vision

Boards was to get a clear picture of our personal and professional goals and to revisit them daily. If you are constantly reminded of your vision, you will start believing in yourself and speaking your goals and vision into existence. The vision board is a collection of words and pictures taped or glued on a poster board, which depicts where you want to be related to your dreams, the goals you want to accomplish, and life, in general. It could be your college choice, ideal job, or career; it could be where you want to vacation, your dream car, etc. There is no "right" or "wrong" with a vision board; its purpose is to provide a glimpse (or in-depth look) into who you are and where you want to be. I asked each player to put together a collage of pictures and words to tell a story about themselves and their ambitions.

During the halfway point of our season, we had a parent dinner at the school, and each player presented their vision. It was exciting, entertaining, and eye opening because some parents did not know that their kid had some of the ideas and thoughts that they shared about their futures. My assistant head coach and I also completed vision boards and shared with the group. This exercise was so much fun and allowed each of us to learn about one another in a very open and relaxed manner.

This team went through so much and put so much effort into a season with minimal complaints, dedicated hearts, that consumed so much time and effort. I did my best to prepare them to be as competitive as possible and in a position to be successful on the court. Adding a robust fellowship component that was intentionally placed into the structure of the program was immeasurable to our overall success.

Ohio State Lady Buckeye Games

"In any given moment we have two options:
To step forward into growth or to step
back into safety."
– Abraham Maslow

The fellowship component took on an added dimension during my first year of coaching until my final year of coaching. We would attend at least one Ohio State Lady Buckeye Basketball game. The goal was two-fold: 1) another opportunity to be together and fellowship; 2) to learn from watching the game of basketball. I am a big believer that watching as much basketball as possible, whether it be in person or on TV, helps the developing player to see things that they would not necessarily see in practice or in their own games. Our girls were able to see the confidence that high-level athletes have, regardless of the situation, how hard they worked on offense and defense, the positive body language (in most cases) that they displayed even during adversity, the tremendous amount of effort they gave on both ends of the court, the leadership they showed on the court and on the bench, and much more. There are so many teaching moments that can be used in their own games just by watching highly skilled athletes play the game. I treated the Lady Bucks game as a required practice and not only were current high school players asked to attend, but I also included their parents as well as all junior high school girls' team members and their parents.

This thought process goes back to the "Future" component of A Players Program, which includes mentorship and involvement of the MCS Junior High School Girls Basketball team. The junior high school and high school girls basketball teams are one program, and I wanted to ensure that this was promoted as much as possible. At the next practice, we intentionally took time to discuss the Lady Buckeye basketball game as far as what they saw, what they learned, as well as other observations that could help our team or themselves. The feedback and attention to detail that were shared was amazing and really showed their desire to get better.

Service Projects and Partnerships

"Vision without action is merely a dream.
Action without vision just passes time. Vision
with action can change the world.
– Joel A. Baker

The Athletic Department at Madison Christian School had an "ask" of each of their coaches and sports programs each year. This was for each of their teams to complete at least one service project during their season. The idea fostered not only team unity, but it was a tool to give back to those who may not be as fortunate as us. It allowed us to give back by simply volunteering our time to assist in any way that we could. We typically completed more than one service project during the season, and during the first two basketball seasons, we completed services related to Meals on Wheels food deliveries, visiting a local assisted living home to play games and chat with the elderly, serving food, washing dishes, sweeping floors at a local pizza restaurant, or attending a literacy event at an elementary school to read to kids. My third season at Madison Christian School was when the service project evolved into a partnership with the Bridgeway Academy and Therapy Center.

The Bridgeway Academy

"We make a living by what we get. We make a life by what we give."
– Winston Churchill

I have a nephew who attends the Bridgeway Academy and Therapy Center. The academy caters to children with special needs (with an emphasis on autism). I initially reached out to Bridgeway to see if our basketball team could offer volunteer services at the school, such as reading or playing games with the kids. They loved the idea, and from there, our partnership grew rapidly. Over the years, the Lady Eagles conducted basketball clinics at the school and offered our time to play games or read to the children. Where the partnership grew was via philanthropic opportunities, in which we raised funds yearly through T-shirt sales, concessions, and ticket gate sales from a special Eagles for a Cause Basketball Game, where Bridgeway and autism awareness were the focus of the event. We also worked together to conduct a Walkathon on the

Bridgeway Academy campus, where proceeds from T-Shirt sales and miles walked were given directly to Bridgeway. The money that was raised by the Lady Eagle basketball program is nothing compared to the heavy donors that give to Bridgeway, but the connection we have with them is fulfilling, and their respectful treatment of us was equal to the treatment given to their larger donors. Our girls were so grateful for the opportunity to serve, and some have been offered summer volunteer internships to assist at the academy.

During the summer of 2022, Bridgeway asked me to give the commencement address to their graduating class. I was incredibly honored to share an uplifting message with six incredibly strong and talented individuals. I had never given a commencement address, so I just spoke from my heart on topics such as adversity, motivation, and moving forward. It was by far one of the most fulfilling moments of my life to speak at this event and something that I will never forget.

Bridgeway Testimonial

In January of 2019, Bridgeway Academy became connected with Madison Christian School athletics - more specifically, the Lady Eagles Basketball Team. At the time, I was new in my role as Communications Manager and had only been at Bridgeway for just over a year. Our partnership with the Lady Eagles was the first relationship at Bridgeway of which I had been able to be a part from the very beginning.

Not too long into the partnership, we experienced challenges as both organizations navigated through the COVID-19 pandemic. Fortunately, we were able to get creative and host different types of events and interactions to keep the partnership moving.

Something I have learned through my many years in fundraising is that people, often with the very best of intentions, will sometimes over-promise a commitment of their time, talent, or treasure. This can put organizations in a position where they must backpedal on plans or make last minute changes when the expectations are unrealistic, causing stress for both parties. Fortunately, the positive, timely, and straightforward communication that we have with Coach Jeff and the Lady Eagles has provided an environment for smooth execution of programs and a mutual reliance on each other for success.

This type of a trust-based collaboration has made us feel like true partners, not just recipients of their charity.

Our partnership with the Lady Eagles has left an indelible impression on myself, the staff, and students at Bridgeway. We have felt like true teammates in the success and development of players' character and the school-wide culture of giving at MCS.

Any time that I can give someone new to Bridge-way the opportunity to interact with our students, it's a win-win. Through our partnership with Coach Jeff and MCS Athletics, our students have had enriching experiences and have made new friends. MCS student-athletes have also had the opportunity to interact and learn from those who are different from themselves.

Janelle Maur (Director of Advancement, Bridgeway Academy & Therapy Center)

It Takes a Village

"The difference between the best and the rest is the work ethic, the belief, the preparation, the skill and the will."

– Jon Gordon

I learned early in my coaching journey that building a program could not be completed by me alone. I was grateful to have an assistant head coach and athletic director who were on the same page as myself in relation to the vision and direction of the team. However, to make the program truly a program, I needed outside help that Madison Christian School could not offer.

My daughter trained with two former Ohio State Lady Buckeyes during the offseason, where she improved in areas such as ball handling, shooting, strength building, confidence, and overall toughness. This was the building block to having them come to the school and train our entire team. Twice a year, I would have a scheduled practice where they would lead practice and provide college-level drills to improve the development and skillset of the team. The girls absolutely loved this! Sometimes, hearing the things that we as coaches say all the time coming from a different voice makes a significant difference and opens the eyes of the girls to execute effectively. The practices with the former Lady Buckeyes were energetic and a fantastic way to provide a "change-up" from the routine grind of practices. Finally, their positive presence led to many players individually working out with them during the offseason. You could just see the growth, development, and confidence of many of the girls during these sessions. It takes a village …

Madison Christian School has an agreement with Ohio Health, where a certified athletic trainer is provided at each sporting event. I decided to use their expertise in multiple ways to add value and help our team. Over the years, I had the trainer or an Ohio Health representative speak to the team on topics such as nutrition, mental health, sports psychology, conditioning, and more. I was a believer that talent can only take you so far and that preparation before, during, and after an event is equally as important to be successful on the court and in life. It takes a village …

I was introduced to a Speed and Agility Coach through my relationship with the former Lady Buckeyes. The incredible high energy of this guy was contagious! I had him come in once during the summer and once at the start of the season to give the girls a thorough workout. He put them through drills that track athletes and football players used to help improve quickness, speed, burst and agility. The girls fed off his approach and put forth some of the best effort that I had seen from them. I saw things that, honestly, I did not know some had in them, and you could truly see the high amount of athleticism coming out that many of them did not know that they had within themselves. It takes a village ...

It was important to share the "village" at Madison Christian. I would routinely invite the junior high school girls basketball team to join in any training or in listening to speakers who came to the school. "A Players Program" does not actually start at the high school level; it starts with the future, and the future is our junior high girls basketball team, who (at some point) will become the present. We also invited the Madison Christian Boys Basketball Team to sessions that were applicable to their interests. High school basketball season is exceptionally long, and when you consider summer practices along with the grueling winter months, basketball consumes five-plus months of the year. Hearing the constant voices of myself and my assistant head coach can become tiresome, and I understand that. Therefore, having fresh voices, new training, and outside motivation was huge for our program and the girls, and their parents appreciated the approach as well. It takes a village ...

The Seasons

*Effort and Attitude – "There are two things in
life of which we have complete control...
Effort and Attitude."*
– Chuck Wilson

I segmented our basketball year into seasons: Summer, Preseason, Regular Season, and Postseason. I also communicated an End of the Season summary once all of the four seasons were completed.

Summer:

This was the time of the year for each player to get fundamentally better at the game of basketball. I was grateful to have an assistant head coach who was a human Google Search for basketball-specific drills and conditioning exercises. The summer was his time to shine. I leaned on him to push and challenge the girls beyond their limits to improve their weaknesses, make them better, and push them on conditioning. OHSAA allowed ten summer sessions, and we usually practiced for two hours per session in the month of June. We tried to make it fun with competitive drills, but everyone knew that this was the time to work and improve (not so much as a team, but individually). I knew that improving individually during the summer would help the team collectively improve when the pre-season and regular season arrived.

Preseason:

The start of official practices around the end of October is the time of the year where we are still putting great emphasis on basketball-related conditioning but also putting in the framework of what we want to do offensively, defensively, with out of bounds plays, press, press breaks, and more. On the very first day of official practice, I addressed the team with an "Is This Program for You" speech that sets the tone as we embark on our journey:

IS THIS PROGRAM FOR <u>YOU</u>?

- Are you excited, fired up, ready to bring a high level of energy and "Juice" beginning today?

- Are you ready for a new season, new goals, new expectations, new highs and some lows?
- Can you transition, learn from the past, learn from mistakes, and demonstrate growth and maturity?
- Can you be coachable, keep an open mind, listen, COMMUNICATE on offense & defense, try different things outside your comfort zone, and incorporate an approach to your game that will improve you?
- Can you be accountable for your actions and responsible for your assignments?
- Are you able to focus and give maximum effort for 90 to 120 minutes of practice and 32 minutes in a game, whether you are on the floor or on the bench?
- Can you remove a poor attitude or poor body language when individual or team adversity strikes?
- Can you learn from your mistake, move forward, and put aside being upset because of a missed shot, a turnover, a defensive lapse, or any mistake that you make?
- Can you be a team player, and can you remove an "it's all about me" mentality?
- Can you encourage your teammates in practice, in the game, and from the bench?
- Can you sit on the bench without an attitude and/or without feeling sorry for yourself because

you made a mistake or because you are not getting the playing time you feel that you are owed?

- Do you want to have fun?
- Do you want to be a part of "A Players Program" that understands our identity, keeps God First, offers Service, recognizes the Past, the Present, the Future and brings the "Juice"?
- Do you want to be a part of a program that has a tremendously long season but is filled with outside activities, fellowship, and periodic speakers that are infused regularly?
- The coaching staff is here for you and will give you all we have. Can you give us the same?

To be clear, these are not rules; they are very simple, common-sense STANDARDS that are non-negotiable. If you cannot meet these STANDARDS, then perhaps this program is not for you.

The preseason sets the stage as to what we will do on the court during the regular season. This is also the time of the year where one-on-one meetings are held with players; team and individual goals and objectives are discussed, and a general plan is put into place. We go hard during the preseason with fast-paced drills and a collective approach to getting as much accomplished as possible in a short amount of time.

Regular Season:

It is "go" time, and the real games begin during the regular season. The infrastructure for what we want to do on the court and the mindset of who we want to be as a team are in place. The mentality of my team was aggressive and fast-paced. We were a pressing team that loved to get up and down the floor quickly and put pressure on the opponent on both ends of the floor. Conditioning and fundamental drills still occur during each practice but are scaled back considerably. For me, it was necessary to have fresh legs during a long season of 20-22 games during the regular season. Practices typically consisted of film study, reviewing areas where we needed to improve offensively and defensively, internal scrimmages where we incorporated everything, many teachable moments, and game planning for the next opponent. I typically scouted the opponent in advance to help our players better prepare for them, and the girls seemed to appreciate having a good understanding of what to expect from the team that they were about to play.

I was a big believer in mental health days when the schedule permitted. For example, if we did not have a game on a Thursday, Wednesday would be an off-day to recharge. High school basketball season is the longest season of any sport at Madison Christian School, and periodic rest days are extremely important for the players' and coaches' mental health and sanity.

Devotionals were a key component of the regular season. They provided a time of reflection, sharing, caring, and (most of all) learning. I asked every player and coach to lead one devotional per season. A devotional could be something that was going on in their lives that tied to a scripture; it could be sharing and discussing their favorite Bible verse, a simple prayer, or anything they really wanted to share or discuss. There was no right or wrong to any devotional that they wanted to share. It was a personal testament that reflected on them individually or collectively as a team. My assistant head coach and I took part in devotionals during our turn just like the rest of the team, and our devotionals usually took the face of what was happening at the time with the team. Adversity was the word or issue that we faced often, and adversity over the years could have been in the form of an injury, game losses, family issues, health, attitude, etc. Below is an outlined example of an interactive devotional that I led related to dealing with adversity.

"The most important thing you will ever do in your life, when given the opportunity, is respond. Everyone gets knocked down, that's not what people remember. They remember what you do about it. Adversity does not

make you a man or woman. It only reveals where you are as a man or woman."
– Coach Matt Deggs

Adversity: Who can define adversity?

- When circumstances or situations work against you, you face *adversity.*
- When things seem against you — circumstances or instances of bad luck — you are facing adversity; a state of misfortune or affliction; unnecessary and unforeseen trouble resulting from an unfortunate event.
- Sometimes, people use the form of the phrase "turning *adversity* into opportunity". This refers to the ability for people to take a tough situation (adversity) and make it into a successful one.

  o On the basketball court how can this be done (turning adversity into success)?
  o Comment: God will help you get through tough times. Sometimes we make it seem as if we are the only ones going through trials. Every Christian has dealt with or is dealing with some type of adversity. It could be persecution, unemployment, family problems, homelessness, financial issues, etc. **Notice a basketball game was not mentioned.**

○ Comment: Always remember that hardships in life make you stronger. Continually pray and commit to the Lord, and He will make your path straight.

Uplifting Scriptures to read during times of adversity:

- Proverbs 24:10: If you faint (falter) on the day of trouble, your strength is small!
- Corinthians 4:8-10: In every way we are troubled, but we are not crushed by our troubles. We are frustrated, but we do not give up.
- Romans 5:3-5: We can rejoice, too, when we run into problems and trials, for we know that they help us develop endurance. Endurance develops strength of character, and character strengthens our confident hope of salvation. And this hope will not lead to disappointment.
- James 1:2: Consider it pure joy, whenever you face trials of many kinds, because you know that the testing of your faith develops perseverance. Perseverance must finish its work so that you may be mature and complete, not lacking anything.

Tips For Overcoming Adversity:

1. Be aware of and accept that adversity is inevitable in life. Adversity is part of life. To avoid or resist it will only make it persist. Everywhere

there are floods, wars, death, tragedy, etc. (**Notice nothing related to a basketball game.**)

2. Build your internal resources. Work on cultivating emotional strength, courage, and discipline.

3. Build your external resources. Build a support system of family and friends.

4. If you do not have enough built-up resilience or experience in dealing with difficulty, adversity can crush you, but if you do have sufficient resilience, then it will make you stronger. How? Resilience, like any muscle; it is built up gradually with repeated exposure to obstacles. If you lack practice in confronting obstacles (such as choosing to avoid them), one traumatic event can take you down.

5. Take inspiration and learn from others who have dealt successfully with adversity. Talk to trusted people within your circle, such as your minister, your parents, older siblings, teachers, coaches, or anyone who can assist with overcoming adversity.

We have had so many amazing devotionals over the years, and we have learned so much from them. We have also shared in the emotions of many of the presenters with tears, laughter, and feelings that we had not felt before. The influence and growth that we all experienced by listening and conducting our devotionals were incredibly inspiring.

Postseason:

The end of the regular season allows us to breathe a bit prior to the commencement of tournament play. Usually there is a seven to ten day gap between the last regular season game and the first tournament game. At the first practice after the final regular season game, I would take this time to meet individually with each player to discuss really anything that was on their mind but also to begin the process of getting them ready for next season (if they are not a senior). I have these discussions now because tournament play will end very abruptly when a loss occurs. When you lose a game in the tournament, your season is over, and there are no more practices nor much communication until the Winter Sports Awards Night. Therefore, it was important to me to set them up for the summer and discuss what they need to work on. My assistant head coach would also review overall team statistics from the regular season and hand out individual player statistics.

I would share my thoughts and (more importantly) have them share their thoughts and provide feedback on the season. The next practice and going forward until the first tournament game was focused on our opponent, whether it be film study or practicing (specifically on how to beat them or fine-tuning what we need to do on both ends of the floor). Losing a tournament game is extremely emotional. We have seniors who have played their last game, and it is the culmination of an exceptionally long season. Many tears are shed; hugs are obtained, but in the end, I am always so proud of the effort and hard work that every single player put into making the season a success on and off the court. Regardless of our win-loss record, every season was successful due to the many things that were accomplished and the growth that each player and coach experienced.

End of Season Summary:

After my first season as coach, I started to write an end of season summary for each individual player, and I would mail them to their homes. The summary consisted of a brief synopsis of the season, the strengths of the player, and areas of improvement which I would like to see them work on during the summer. Areas of improvement could consist of fundamentals, on-court actions or attitude and mental tenacity. I was very direct and transparent in this summary and made sure that each player and parent was clear on the areas of improvement. What was amazing to me was the positive responses of the players to my feedback. For some, we could see immediate improvement, and for others, the improvement may have taken two to three years to become apparent. I did not care how long it took because all I could ever ask for was effort, maturity, and growth.

Captains

"The mediocre leader tells. The good leader explains. The superior leader demonstrates. The great leader inspires."
– Gary Patton

I am big on leadership. It is important to prepare our children to be leaders at home, in school, in athletics, and in the workplace. I personally tried to be the best leader that I could be and to set an example for the girls as they went about their daily lives. I even brought outside influences to share their leadership techniques and examples for the girls to follow. One of those speakers happened to be one of my daughters who received her master's degree in Higher Education and started her own consulting firm, where she shared leadership principles. She presented best practices and techniques that related to being a strong leader to both the boys' and girls' basketball teams. It was another example as to why it takes a village to have a successful program.

I did not take captain selections lightly. It was important that my captains were joined at the hip with me, as well as the vision and direction of the program. I needed to have trust in the captains because, at times, I needed to share things with them that I could not share with anyone else except them. I also wanted them to share things with me, knowing that they could trust me with information, especially if it was related to specific team members. I empowered the captains to take charge of the team, lead the team, meet with the team, listen to them, and provide feedback to them (individually or as a group) where needed. The captains whom I chose also had a mix of "lead by example" and/or "lead vocally", when necessary, and they leveraged their strengths for the betterment of the team. I was extremely blessed to have had a strong group of captains during my nine-year tenure at the school.

Wednesday Juice

"More than that, we REJOICE in our SUFFERING, knowing that suffering produces ENDURANCE, and endurance produces CHARACTER, and character produces HOPE, and hope does not put us to shame, because God's LOVE has been poured into our HEARTS through the Holy Spirit who has been given to us."

– Romans 5:3-5

Wednesday Juice was inspired by a friend of mine who has posted "Monday Motivations" on social media platforms for many years. His words would get my week off to a positive start, and they were simple, concise, and straight-to-the-point. When I started coaching, I knew that I wanted to do something similar, but I certainly did not want to infringe on his positive reinforcement on Mondays. Therefore, I decided to provide energy, motivation, affirmation, and "juice" on Wednesdays via Instagram and Facebook. My primary audience for the posts were the students at Madison Christian School and, of course, anyone else who found inspiration from the posts. In most cases, I would post early in the morning on Wednesdays, usually by 6:00 AM, because I wanted the audience to start their day with Wednesday Juice before they went to school or work.

Wednesday Juice could be in the form of a statement such as "Never discourage anyone who continually makes progress, no matter how slow," to something uplifting such as "You don't need a new day to start over; you only need a new mindset." I used Wednesday Juice to intentionally address a loss on the court or to say something uplifting from a situation that happened during a game, practice, or with a specific player. Wednesday Juice came during the middle of week when we all needed some type of "pick me up" to keep us moving forward. It provided assurances, reminders, and even reinforcement in relation to things that may have been going on in our lives. Wednesday Juice has taken on a life of its own, continues each Wednesday, and many readers really look forward to Wednesdays to see what the topic of the week will be. Each chapter of this book begins with a "Wednesday Juice"; below are some more of my favorites.

- *"Forgive others, not because they deserve forgiveness, but because you deserve peace." – Johnathan Lockwood Huie*

- *"Strength does not come from winning. Your struggles develop your strength. When you go through hardships and decide not to surrender, that is strength." – Mahatma Gandhi*
- *"If you do not acknowledge mistakes, you cannot learn from them. Making mistakes does not show weakness; however, failing to recognize and improve from mistakes does. Continue down the path of growth." – Coach Jeff Howell*
- *"Positive people focus on the purpose not the circumstance." – Justin Forsett*
- *"You either get bitter or you get better. It is that simple. You either take what has been dealt to you and allow it to make you a better person, or you allow it to tear you down. The choice does not belong to fate, it belongs to you." – Josh Shipp*
- *"We want better, but we do not want to go through nothing to get … better" Pastor Dale Tucker, Sr.*
- *"Leaders who do not listen will eventually be surrounded by people who have nothing to say." – Andy Stanley*
- *"Ability is what you are capable of doing. Motivation determines what you do. Attitude determines how well you do it." – Lou Holtz*
- *"What you get by achieving your goals is not as important as what you become by achieving your goals." – Henry David Thoreau*

Senior Night: February 3, 2018

"Optimism is the faith that leads to achievement. Nothing can be done without hope and confidence."

– Helen Keller

"Believe in yourself and all that you are. Know that there is something inside you that is greater than any obstacle."

– Christian D. Larson

Just reflecting on this day brings out emotions that I still feel and will never forget. I have had many successes on the court with wins and off the court with player growth and maturity; however, there is nothing that quite measures up to this night.

Shekinah Christian had been a powerhouse school in the conference, the district, and the state for several years, and 2018 was no different. We went to their place and lost by 25+ points on a Saturday afternoon earlier in the season. I lost my mind after the game and really let the team "have it" (by raising my voice at them) for their lack of effort. I was telling them that they seemed defeated as soon as they got to the school parking lot ... and more. I was beside myself, but when I calmed down, I found a scripture to post on social media that night for them to see; it was both calming and inspirational: "Be strong! Be fearless!! Don't be afraid and don't be scared by your enemies, because the Lord your God is the one who marches with you. He won't let you down, and he won't abandon you." Deuteronomy 31:6

Fast forward ... I have always made it known to the athletic department that I would prefer Senior Nights under my tenure to be on a weekend night (Friday or Saturday). It was important to have as many family members and friends as possible at this event to support and recognize our amazing seniors. It just so happened that the final weekend home game that year was against Shekinah Christian. Senior night is traditionally versus a team whom the home team would have a good chance of winning and an opportunity to have some fun playing against. I looked at other game nights, such as a Tuesday or Thursday, around that time, and while there were teams available whom we kind of knew we could beat, the fact of the matter was that a Tuesday or Thursday crowd would be smaller; the student section would be lighter, and many family members from out of town would not be able to attend. Therefore, I went with Saturday, February 3, 2018, against Shekinah Christian.

When I shared with the girls when Senior Night would be and against whom, there were a lot of groans and disgust among them. My daughter was one of the senior captains, and she would come home from school and tell me that the other three seniors were "pissed." Frankly, even the athletic director, my assistant head coach, and some parents questioned the decision of playing that team on Senior Night. However, I stuck with my decision because (regardless of the outcome) the opportunity for family and friends, who have never seen those seniors play a game, would have been missed.

A week prior to Senior Night, I went to work on the girls from a mental standpoint, and my assistant head coach and I went to work on a game plan for this game. Mentally, Wednesday Juice became Monday, Tuesday, Thursday, and Friday Juice. I was posting motivational and reflective quotes on social media, and I was also sending Bible verses and inspirational content to them via text for the entire week. We knew that Shekinah was a very good outside shooting team and did not look to score near the basket as much as they preferred to shoot three-point shots. Therefore, with a defender in the face of whomever had the ball, we came up with an extended zone defense that would force them into shooting longer than usual and lower percentage shots. However, leading up to gameday, there were still some folks looking at me sideways and questioning my decision.

> *"I focus on this one thing: forgetting the past and looking forward to what lies ahead...."*
> *– Philippians 3:13*

It was a packed gym on gameday. All sections of the bleachers were full, and the student section was rocking. We had four, fabulous seniors who were recognized before the game with their families, and many of their extended family, who had never seen them play, were in attendance. My mission, in that respect, was accomplished. Since my daughter was one of the seniors, we had family members from multiple states in town and so many family members and friends from the Columbus area and around Ohio who made the trip for this one game. It was a very emotional time for my wife and me. Seeing our daughter recognized and walking across the floor with her for the final time at a home game was tough emotionally, and the game had not even started.

I gathered the team together after the brief ceremony, and I summarized the game plan again. I hyped them up with a whole lot of "juice"; we prayed, and we hit the floor for pregame warmup. I was so fired up; the team was ready, and the crowd was incredibly electric. We came out in the first quarter as though we were shot out of a cannon, and in the first four minutes, we were up 16-4. Shekinah called timeout, and the crowd was going crazy! The players were excited, and I was jumping and hollering as if I was out of my mind. In the huddle, my assistant head coach simply said, "Okay, everyone, just breathe; you too, Coach!"

We played the best defense that I have ever seen us play, scored in ways that I could never imagine, and BEAT Shekinah Christian 58-43 on Senior Night!!! Yep, I broke down emotionally like a baby. The weight of playing this team on this night was heavy on my heart, and I cried big tears. However, in the end, as is the case with everything that we seek in this program, there were life lessons that revolved around believing in ourselves, trust, preparation, effort, and accomplishment after you take care of what you need to take care of. That day is a memory that will forever live within me and will forever be a teaching moment. To this day, I have former players on that team share with me that their basketball Senior Night was and still is the most exciting and most memorable experience of their young lives.

The End of an Era

"Everyday focus on your purpose. Remember why you do what you do. We do not get burned out because of what we do. We get burned out because we forget why we do it."
— *Jon Gordon*

March 10, 2022

Athletic Director,

This correspondence will serve as my formal notification that the 2022-23 basketball season will be my final season as Head Coach of the Madison Christian Lady Eagle Varsity Basketball Team.

It has been an honor, joy, and privilege to coach all the student-athletes in our program from Year 1 to what will be Year 9 next season. I am grateful to you for taking a chance and giving me this opportunity, and I am also thankful for all the support from the athletic department, school, parents, players, and most of all God for placing me in the right situation at the right time.

If you permit, I would like to continue not only being an ambassador of Madison Christian School but also expanding my scope of player, skill, and leadership development to all grades - boys and girls of MCS - through group and individual skill sessions, camps, and clinics. At your convenience, let us further discuss thoughts and ideas related to my role upon completion of the 2022-23 basketball season.

I appreciate you, and I cannot thank you enough for allowing me to grow spiritually and for placing me in a position to make a difference in the lives of these young ladies over the years.

Sincerely,
Jeff Howell

This was tough. As a coach, there is never a right time to make this decision. When you have invested so much time, energy, and resources into something that you genuinely believe in, letting it go is hard. What made it even more difficult was that I had four incredible juniors who would be seniors after this upcoming season. I felt I would be letting them down because I would not be on the sideline to finish out with them. However, as a coach, when is the right time? If you are doing the things that a coach should be doing with a program and parent/player relationships, where seeds have been planted in elementary school to now, there will never be a right time, and feelings will be hurt.

I knew that I was letting that junior class down, and although they may not have said it to me directly, I could sense their disappointment. The current senior group was fine; they were done after the upcoming season anyway, but as for the juniors, I needed to reach out to them individually and share my decision. After I communicated to the juniors and seniors individually, I addressed the entire team in a letter that I mailed to them and their parents. In the letter, I explained that, frankly, I was tired and wanted the freedom to spend time with grandkids, who live out of state, without the commitment of a practice or game interfering with family time.

I addressed my decision in the letter and promised that I would address it only one more time on the first official day at practice, and from that point on, it would not be addressed again until the end of the season. I made a promise that this decision was not going to be a distraction, and the focus would be all about the current three seniors and the season at hand.

The Final Season: 2022-23

In David's day "the King's business required haste" (1 Sam.21:8). The King's business was urgent. Urgent is interpreted as pressing, calling for immediate attention, now! The King's business is different from the business of an ordinary subject. It is pressing, it calls for immediate attention, and it demands high priority. It is urgent!
– The Holy Bible, King James Version

Summer practices were back to normal with fundamental skill development. The year before, we played in a summer league with five other teams, which provided an enjoyable way to play competitive games twice weekly during the summer and get away from the usual summer regime. The league disbanded, and we were back to our normal practice of skill development and scrimmages during the month of June. Due to having a veteran team with three seniors and four juniors, we added more elements that summer in relation to offensive and defensive philosophy that we would be executing during the regular season. This would really allow us to hit the ground running when real practices began in the Fall.

As preseason practices began, we had an offsite, overnight retreat in early November for the second year in a row. I got the idea from the Madison Christian Boys' Program, who for years had an overnight retreat in a cabin in the woods. I loved the idea, but there was no way that I was going into the woods to stay overnight. Therefore, I decided that we were going to have a retreat at a Hilton location, where I had a cousin who was the general manager. On Day 1 (Saturday) of the previous year, we went to Dave & Busters for a few hours and came back to the hotel for food and team building games. Another cousin, who was on the 2002 Ohio State Football National Championship team under Coach Jim Tressel, spoke and really got us motivated for the season.

The next morning (Sunday), we had individual devotionals; team captains were selected, and I spoke on team goals and objectives. Parents picked up their girls around noon on Sunday, and we left refreshed and ready to start the new season. The fun that we had together, the devotionals that we heard, the prayer that we had, the bonding via team building games, and of course, all the food that we ate were incredible. Having this type of outing prior to the regular season was the foundation of learning about one another, having fellowship together, and building trust. It was substantial for our mindsets and made the beginning of the new season much more relaxing and focused on the task.

One thing that I was very intentional about was making sure that room assignments were not composed of their best friends. I purposely mixed the freshmen with a senior room leader or placed a vocal type of personality with a personality that was quiet in nature. During lights out, I wanted them to converse and get to know one another. I also gave them a homework assignment during their room time that would encourage conversation and allow them to learn about each other. This was shared with the group on the next morning. If I have one regret about my coaching career, it was the fact that I did not think of doing a retreat, such as this, with our girls much sooner as opposed to the final two years of my tenure. Below was the agenda outline for our final overnight retreat during the 2022-23 basketball season:

Lady Eagles Retreat Agenda

Saturday: Nov 5

- 12:30PM - Penn & Beech Candle Co. - 646 High Street, Worthington OH 43085 - (We will start promptly!)

- Lunch at Dewey's Pizza (next door) while candles are finishing.

  - 640 High Street, Worthington OH 43085

- 3:15PM (approximate) – Hotel Arrival
- Home2Suites (Polaris)

  - 9101 Lyra Dr. Columbus OH 43240

- 4PM-4:30PM: Intro (questions, food, bathrooms)/Team Building Game - NO PHONES
- 4:30PM-5PM: MCS Alumni Discussion
- 5PM-6:20PM: Speaker: Mental Toughness
- 6:20PM-6:30PM: Break
- 6:30PM-7PM: Team Building Games
- 7PM-8PM: Speaker: Former Ohio Dominican University WBB Player and Athletic Hall of Famer
- 8PM-11PM: Team Building Games/Free Time/Individual Coach Meeting (Goals & Expectations)
- 11PM: Lights Out!

Sunday: Nov 6

- 8:30AM-9AM: Breakfast (Hotel provides)
- 9AM-9:30AM: Room Assignment Discussion
- 9:30AM-10:15AM: Individual/Team Devotions
- 10:15AM-11AM: Coach's Discussion/Captain Announcement

- 11AM-11:20AM: Team Building Game
- 11:20AM-12PM: Team Tik Tok Creation
- 12PM: Parent Pick-up

Food, snacks, water, and Gatorade will be available throughout the weekend.

Room Assignments:
Room 1:

  (Room Leader)
  Player
  Player
  Player

Room 2:

  (Room Leader)
  Player
  Player
  Player

Room 3:

  (Room Leader)
  Player
  Player
  Player

The Penn & Beech Candle outing was extremely fun. The team, parents, and a few alumni joined as we chose from many scents, mixed them together, and made our own candles. We had great team bonding, laughs, and even some competition as to whose candle smelled the best.

Every season, we would have a team word and tie it to a Biblical verse related to that word. During the retreat and for my final season, our word was "Urgency". Honestly, I wish that I would have chosen this word years earlier and stuck with the word throughout my career. During the summer leading up to the season, everyone knew that this, in fact, was my final season and that 2022-23 was also the finale for three seniors. Therefore, I wanted to articulate a word that created immediate attention or action, today and right now! It was **urgent** that every single player and coach do their best in practice, which would translate to success on game days. Although the word "urgency" was a team word, the word silently applied for those seniors and me. We wanted to have the best season possible and the most fun that we ever had while winning a lot of games at the same time, and the urgency was now! Boy was that mission accomplished during the 2022-23 season.

The season overall was phenomenal; we finished with the most wins in school history (since eclipsed by the 2023-24 team), beat our rival (Tree of Life) for the first time in several years, won our Senior Night game, and won in the first round of the OHSAA tournament in overtime. I was incredibly surprised during senior night festivities when my wife spear-headed a surprise to honor me during the festivities and coordinated a dinner after our game. I knew that something was up when my two older daughters showed up as well as many family members from everywhere, in state and out of state. It felt like Senior Night 2018 all over again with the electricity in the gym. The night was amazing for me and the three seniors.

There could not have been a better storybook ending to the season and my coaching career. We had an incredible win-loss record, a postseason win, multiple players on the All-League Team, one of my juniors named District 10 and Division IV Player of the Year, myself being named conference (MOCAL) Coach of the Year and District 10-Division IV Coach of the Year, a positive send off for the seniors, and finally, an incredible amount of fun! I cannot express my gratitude enough for everyone involved for an amazing 2022-23 basketball season.

The Past: Lady Eagle Alumni

*"What you get by achieving your goals is
not as important as what you become
by achieving your goals."*
– Henry David Thoreau

When you graduate from the Lady Eagle basketball program, you do not go away. The "Past" component of "A Players Program" is triggered once your senior season ends. I encourage as much involvement as possible from our alumni as far as practicing with us, being a part of my summer basketball camps, attending games and off court activities, and praying with and for us. Alumni have an open door invitation to join us as much as they want to join us, and I am appreciative when they do. A few will even come back and participate in practices with us. This is huge and really pushes current team members to work even harder.

One year, we had an Alumni vs Present Team game that we advertised and treated like a real game with officials. We had a nice crowd of parents, students and MCS staff who attended. It was so much fun, and the Alumni still had some skills that they displayed! I continue to support and check in on many former Lady Eagles when they go off to college, and I love to attend events that they are a part of when my schedule permits. One thing that I make sure that they know is that I am always there for them and will always support them as they continue their life journey. Whether it is a reference letter for a job or just to connect and catch-up, I consider myself their forever Coach and will help and assist in any way that I can.

All nine teams were uniquely different. However, the common qualities that all nine teams possessed were effort, determination, and a desire to grow and get better. These ladies accepted coaching, accepted challenges, and pulled together in good times and when adverse situations arose. They were my extended family, I am thankful, and I love each one of them as if they were my own.

Being a Great Teammate

"Talent is God given, Be Humble. Fame is man-given, Be Grateful. Conceit is self-driven, Be Careful."
– John Wooden

After my first year as head coach, I found a great article from the Basketball for Coaches website www.basketballforcoaches.com and Coach Mac, titled "23 Qualities of a Great Teammate." It is a phenomenal article and serves as a reminder to the little things that are required with not only being a great teammate but also to maintain a positive culture now and into the future. I was a big believer that the little things that a freshman, sophomore, and junior learned through their experiences as a part of "A Players Program" would continue to the next group of girls coming in behind them. The upper-class students would complement my efforts to promote the program vocally through their actions by conducting themselves in the right way. Exhibiting the qualities to being a great teammate becomes muscle memory when you consistently put it into practice daily. Many of these qualities not only help in the game of basketball but also as these girls move to the next level of their lives, such as college and career advancement; they will use many of these qualities on a regular basis. Below, I share my personal Top 10 of the "23 Qualities of Being a Great Teammate" along with some thoughts.

1) A great teammate develops real relationships with their teammates:

There is that word again, "relationships". Players being intentional with getting to know their teammates on and off the court and building those relationships is a key component to growth and trust. Adversity and losses on the court will no doubt occur at some point, but you always win when friendships and a genuine enjoyment of one another is the foundation of the program.

2) A great teammate is willing to play any role on the team:

A good coach should always place the team and player in the best possible position to be successful. Communicating the role of each player should be done effectively and often. I had a player whose role during her first three seasons was as the defensive specialist. I would routinely have her guard the opponent's best player because she was my best defender. Her offense was not up to par during those early seasons, but during her senior year, she maintained her defensive prowess and added an element of scoring consistently on offense. Understanding your role, continuing to improve while maintaining a team-first attitude are important qualities to being a great teammate.

3) A great teammate works hard to improve their game:

Whether it is academics, athletics, work, home, or life, to get better, you must put in the time and effort. Committing yourself to getting better will improve your talents individually and translate to team improvement as well. This is an important lead-by-example approach, and teammates will want to mimic your direction and improve as well. When you can collectively have everyone working hard to improve their game, the team and the culture become dynamic, unstoppable and will thrive.

4) A great teammate always leads by example:

On the court, off the court, at the mall, at a restaurant, at home, or wherever you are, leading by example with non-verbal communication and with actions is huge. Putting forth effort, listening to coaches, following directions, having a good attitude, and being prepared are all great components of leading by example. Teammates see this and will follow the example you have intentionally set.

5) A great teammate always has a positive and energetic attitude:

For me, this is one of the most important qualities. Regardless of the score, playing time concerns, bad practice or game, or any other adverse situations, having a positive and energetic mindset is contagious toward their teammates. In my work life in sales, I run into objections daily, but I must put those objections aside and move to the next deal and the next deal and the next deal until the timing is right when I get a deal closed. A positive, energetic mindset has helped me to be successful in my coaching career as well as in my job.

These quotes are impactful:

"Promise to be just as enthusiastic about the success of others as you are about your own."
— *John Wooden.*

"I am looking for players who make their teammates better. You do that with enthusiasm and passion."
— *Mike Krzyzewski*

6) A great teammate will hold themselves and others accountable to the commitment they made to the team:

This is not easy. It is not easy to admit mistakes or faults; however, with growth, the mature teammates will hold themselves accountable for their actions, as well as hold others accountable for their actions. This is the sign of a good leader and (honestly from my perspective) a future captain. There are times (five to be exact in my nine-year coaching career) that I held myself accountable for getting a technical foul and giving away points from free throws that were made due to my error in judgment. I apologized to the team for my actions because I was wrong. If a player is being lazy or obviously not giving full effort, I would have no problem with a teammate letting them know that they need to step up. Accountability and trust on the court are two very important components to being successful on the court. If everyone is accountable for executing their assignment and teammates trust that you will do so on a consistent basis, more wins than losses will undoubtedly occur, setting the team up for a successful season.

7) A great teammate understands how to deliver praise and criticism:

This is a sensitive quality, and a lot of things come into play; tone of voice, approach, body language, etc., all come into play. With my teams, many were afraid to criticize because they felt that they would lose a friend or be talked about at school. Praising and encouraging a teammate was easy and never an issue, but during adverse times, such as consecutive losses or a poor practice, having someone step up with constructive criticism of the team or an individual player was welcomed by me. I was grateful in most years to have a group of captains who were not afraid to offer criticism when warranted whether it be during a game, in practice or during lunch at school. Hearing criticism from the coach does not resonate as much as it does when you hear the same criticism from a teammate. This was powerful, and you could see and feel better results when a teammate stepped in constructively to voice their concerns.

Below is a notable example of one of my passionate players who criticized a teammate on the court for not putting forth the best effort on a particular play. The passionate player, who criticized her teammate, then sent a text to the entire team and coaches (later that evening), apologizing and taking accountability for her actions. This is one of the most gratifying actions by one of my players that I experienced as a coach:

"Hey guys, I would like to apologize for my actions tonight. They were not appropriate, nor did they represent the Christ like values of this team. It was never my intention and never will be, to tear down any teammate. My intention was to encourage us to keep fighting and hustling, but the manner that I took was extremely unacceptable. We were all trying our best and we played a well fought game today. Tonight, I reflect on my actions and think about the negative effects I had on my teammates and the peers around me and how much tone matters when trying to encourage and constructively criticize others. Again, I am deeply sorry, and I sincerely hope that this will never happen again, whether it be by me or any other teammate. I promise that I will learn from my mistake and continue this season with a more uplifting and positive attitude. I do not want this season to put any more stress on me or you all so I will work harder to make the game of basketball more fun for myself and for all of you. I hope that you ladies have a great night. Continue to Bring the Juice Lady Eagles!!"

"Your words have the power to hurt, to heal, open minds, open hearts and change the world. Never forget the responsibility you have over the words you speak."

– Steve Aitchison

8) A great teammate is willing to accept feedback from their teammates:

I will take it a step further; a great coach is willing to accept feedback from their assistant coach. If you are not learning, you are not growing, and feedback, regardless how critical it may be, is imperative to growth in anything that you do in life. I tried to teach the girls the art of constructive feedback; in other words, I wanted them to see that you can mention a positive in the same sentence as a negative, which helps minimize the defensiveness that a person may feel from critical feedback. I promoted feedback from my teams, and it made for open communication, honesty, transparency, and a comfortable environment to share.

9) A great teammate is dependable, honest, and trustworthy:

Reliability and honesty equal trust. A teammate must be at practices ready to improve and at games ready to play; they must know their assignment on the floor offensively and defensively. A teammate must communicate to the coach or an upper-classmen if they do not know or understand something related to execution. You hear the phrase "trust your teammates", sometimes, and that is what teammates must do to be successful on the court.

Teammates must be able to trust that they are in the right spot on offense to score or on defense to get a stop. Commitment is another way to earn trust because if a player is committed to getting better in the offseason or committed to showing up on time and ready to go for practices or games, these lead-by-example qualities earn a high level of trust in their teammates.

This is a perfect quote by Phil Jackson, "Good teams become great teams when the members trust each other enough to surrender the "me" for the "we."

10) A great teammate constantly encourages their teammates:

This was big for me. I promoted encouragement in practice, during pregame warmups, during games, and after games. We were an encouraging team throughout my years as head coach and did all we could to uplift a teammate, especially during adverse times. Encouragement for me brought energy, changed mindsets, and helped players to perform better. Encouraging one another to push harder during those tough summer and preseason conditioning practices and keeping everyone loose and relaxed prior to and during the games not only brought a lot of energy but it also worked to bring a calming effect to the team. My teams fed off of energy, and encouragement was a foundational component of the "juice."

My Key Components To Program Success

"Success consists of going from failure to failure without loss of enthusiasm."
– Winston Churchill

In no order of priority, below is an aggregate of what worked for me during my 9-year career as the Head Girls' Basketball Coach at Madison Christian School.

- Passion: I was engulfed by the desire to do all that I could, schematically on the court to win games, and to take advantage of the many fellowship opportunities that I wanted to do off the court. I had little regard for the amount of time or energy required of me to be successful. My passionate commitment to the girls, the program and to the school was genuine. I did not want to fail, and when I did fall short at times, I beat myself up for the failure and did all I could to learn and fix going forward.

- Relationships: Getting to know the players and their families personally is extremely huge! Being able to relate to them, knowing their likes and dislikes, understanding what they want to do in the future, as well as knowing what motivates them are all important. I wanted to be able to have conversations that were not always basketball-related but life-related and to offer my feedback based on my own personal or life experiences.

- Transparency: As a coach, it was important for me to be open, honest, and direct. There was nothing to hide in relation to my communication as to what needed to be done as a team or for an individual player. I was clear in team meetings, one-on-one discussions and via their end of the season written summaries of what the goals and objectives were. Players and parents advised me on many occasions how much they appreciated the open, honest, and direct approach. I had one parent jokingly call the End of the Season Summary for her daughter a "performance review"! I never looked at it like that nor was it my objective, but thinking it through, she was correct!

- Coaching Is A Ministry Not An Income Source: Money was never a motivation with me as a coach, and honestly, it should not be at the high school level for any coach. There are many coaches who take this role as a supplementary income source and move around from school to school chasing a dollar. There are also coaches who aspire to move up the ladder to become a high-level Division 1 High School Coach or ultimately ascend to being a college coach. If that is a coach's motivation, I find this to be admirable, and they are fulfilling their ambition. For me, my motivation was simply building a program with a positive culture and experiences that would translate to the growth and development of the student-athlete on and off the court at Madison Christian School. My role afforded me with a pulpit, which allowed me to facilitate the plan that I desired at the only school that I desired to execute this plan.

- Giving Back: When we prayed prior to taking the floor on game days, I always expressed our thankfulness for allowing us the opportunity to play the game of basketball. Not everyone has this opportunity. This is why the Bridgeway Academy partnership is so important because it opens our eyes and our hearts to see how blessed we are to be able to proficiently dribble, shoot and pass the basketball at an elevated level.

Spending time with students who have special needs paints a perspective on life that our players and coaches will cherish and be thankful to have for a lifetime.

- Encourage Player Feedback And Suggestions: Our program was never a controlling program. There are some coaches who will take a "this is how it is going to be done and you will either like the way it is done, or you can leave" approach. Nope! Feedback, suggestions, ideas, and thoughts are welcome and encouraged. As coaches, we do not know everything, nor can we see all that is happening on the court; we cannot get the vibe of players off the court. Empowering captains and players to provide feedback at practices, during games, or at any time is critical and encourages an environment where everyone is respected and embraced; it also encourages open dialogue from all.

- Finding The Right Assistant Coach: I was blessed to have an assistant who had the same priorities and goals that I had. Our relationship and approach worked extremely well for the team. It is vital to have an assistant who does not have an ego, who will push back when needed, and who is not afraid to share thoughts and ideas that will make the team better. A head coach cannot have an ego, should welcome this approach, and empower his assistant.

- Communication: I was never afraid to over communicate. If a player received a text, the parent was copied on the same text. When the team received updates related to practices, games, or other events, the parent was copied on the same text. When the player received their end of season summary in the mail, the parent was included on the envelope as "c/o". There was never, ever any doubt as to what was going on with the team from the individual player or parent. Communication translates to positive relationships and equals success in a variety of fashions.

- Open Door Policy: I was open to having conversations on any day, at any time, at any place with a player or parent. When it was a tough conversation with a player (e.g., playing time), I would always include the parent so that we were all on the same page and so that there would be no miscommunication when the player translated the information that was discussed back to the parent. I also encouraged parents to visit a practice or multiple practices at any time. Some coaches do not like this approach, but I had nothing to hide. This accomplishes a few things: 1) having the parents see for themselves why their daughter may not be getting the playing time that they think she deserves; 2) makes playing time conversations much easier to discuss if the issue does arise; 3) allows parents to see for themselves the type of effort their kid is giving in practices and their interactions with the team; 4) presenting what we as a team are doing in practices to get better overall. Again, I encouraged parents to come check us out.

- Make It Fun And Bring The Juice: Energy is contagious, and I did all I could to bring high energy to every practice, game, and off-court activity. At the end of every practice, we would shoot half court shots, and oh boy, if someone made that shot, I would go crazy jumping up and down and shouting as loud as I could. Of course, when it came time to learn, to understand, and to execute whatever concept we were working on at the time to win games, we were focused, but we had fun, which made the learning environment much more enjoyable to all.

- The Coach Never Stops Learning: I attended several coaches' clinics yearly. Typically, I attended at least one national clinic out of state and two local clinics in Columbus, Ohio. I was constantly trying to collect small nuggets of information from other coaches in relation to their approach, culture, offensive or defensive concepts, etc. I enjoyed attending other games in the Central Ohio area, regardless if it was boys or girls games; I just wanted to watch coaches and their teams and learn from their successes.

I would intentionally get to games early just to watch their pregame warm-up to see if there was something I could take back and incorporate into our pregame. Watching other coaches during games, their sideline mannerisms, and how they managed adversity was extremely helpful to me.

- Reflection: At the end of the season, I would put much thought into what went right, what went wrong, what I could change, what I or the team could improve on, how I could make this team better for the future, etc. There are so many moving parts to a basketball season, and sometimes when adversity or losses occur, you must pivot and try something different. Reflection allows you to process those pivots and determine what should stick and what should be thrown away. Reflections also included conversations with my assistant head coach and determining together areas for improvement and things to add, delete or change for the new season. Taking the time for self and team assessments is critical to long-term success and to ensure growth for all who are involved in the program.

I Am Grateful ...

I have had so many beautiful words from parents, players, and coaches shared over the nine-year span of leading this program that is very flattering and very much appreciated. Their words serve as confirmation that the approach and model that I used for my teams at this school was the correct direction to take. Below are examples of feedback that I have received:

- "Coach, thank you so much!! And thank you for everything you have done for me, and for helping me achieve my goal of playing basketball in college. You have made such an impact on my life, and I am so grateful."
- "Coach, thanks again for another wonderful opportunity to include our daughter. We are so grateful that you have been around to support her passion."
- "Dear Coach Jeff, I do not know how I could thank you enough for all that you have done for

me through all my high school years! You have been a #1 supporter and you have taught me so much about how to take life and keep pushing through it! Thank you so much for teaching me how to be a good leader. Not only did this help me in all my sports but it has helped me through all the different challenges that life has thrown at me. The last four years of basketball have consisted of all my favorite high school memories, and I would not want it any other way. I cannot wait to come back and help with future teams. I wish you the best of luck next season! Love you Coach, thank you again for all that you do."

- "Dear Coach Howell, thank you for inviting me to the Eagles for a Cause game today and being a special guest on the bench with the team. I love that you are a good coach and I love how the team made me feel welcome. I cannot wait to come to your summer camp again and I cannot wait to come to another one of your games. Today I learned that you should have great sportsmanship and a good attitude while playing sports as well as putting in lots of effort. I love the cheat sheet of plays that you gave me to look at while the team was playing, and I even saw a play that my 4th grade team did. Even though the team did not win today I saw lots of good shots, passes and layups. Please tell the team that they did amazing!"

- "We in the athletic department are excited to share that Coach Jeff Howell has been announced as one of the final nominees for The Leadership Playbook Coach of the Year for 2022-2023. The award seeks to honor coaches who maximize success, value growth, and make a positive impact on those they are entrusted to lead. Jamy Bechler, a former college basketball coach and high school athletic director, developed the program. Bechler is now a professional speaker and team performance consultant who hosts a podcast and has written several leadership related books. "We are thrilled to recognize Coach Howell as an example of what a coach should be," said Bechler. "The late Billy Graham used to say that a coach can impact more young people in one year than most people do in a lifetime, and I believe that to be true. No coach is perfect, and the job can be very demanding, but the best coaches try to make situations and other people better. Congratulations, Coach Howell!"
- The definition of Coach Jeff, "the coach who always believes in you and pushes you to do better." Thanks Coach!
- "Hey Coach, our daughter had her first practice tonight for the 4th grade travel basketball team in Pickerington. In the car home. She said she missed you. She was comparing coaches, and the new coach was not measuring up to you.

Nothing against him, you just clearly set the bar high. She said she loved how you saw something in her and pushed her. I just wanted to share and say thank you for being so good at what you do. You have made an impact. I would love to have her still under your leadership somehow one day!"

- "Thank you, Jeff. You are a mentor, leader, and coach to my girl that she will forever hold in her character."

- "Coach, you are so appreciated for going above and beyond the duty. What you are doing for these kids is bigger than basketball."

- "Coach, thank you for being such a pillar of guidance in my daughter's life. I truly appreciate everything that you do. You planted a seed in her early on and you have watched it grow. Thank you!"

"A great coach doesn't just accept who and where you are – they push you to become who you are meant to be so you can go where you are meant to go. When your coach pushes you, pulls you and holds you accountable, it is because they see more in you, and they take their responsibility to bring it out of you seriously. It is because they care about you and your future."

– Coach's Diary

About the Author

Jeff Howell is a multifaceted leader driven by his passion for developing young minds and preparing them fundamentally on the basketball court and off, with life lessons and experiences that will enhance the next phases of their growth. With nearly two decades as a certified Ohio High School basketball official and nine years as the Head Girls Coach at Madison Christian School, Jeff brings a wealth of knowledge, experiences, as well as a direct and transparent approach to his teachings.

More than just a coach, Jeff sees himself as a mentor, leader, and an extension of the family unit that transcends the boundaries of the court. His approach is rooted in a fundamental understanding of the game and meticulously building physical and mental skills from the ground up while challenging his players to push beyond their perceived limits.

Jeff's dedication to his craft is matched only by his devotion to his family. A husband of 34 years and a father of three amazing girls, he seamlessly weaves his family values into his coaching philosophy, providing a holistic experience that nurtures both athletic and personal development.

Off the court, Jeff's achievements are equally impressive. Holding a Bachelor's and Master's degree in Business Administration with an emphasis on Leadership from the Ohio Dominican University, he serves as the Director of National Sales with Cascade365 Liquidity Solutions, demonstrating his ability to excel and provide valuable solutions in a challenging and diverse marketplace.

A diehard Ohio State Buckeyes fan, Jeff's passion for women's basketball extends beyond the sidelines by being a 20+ year season ticket holder for Lady Buckeye basketball. His lifelong allegiance to the Pittsburgh Steelers, despite growing up near Cincinnati, Ohio, further exemplifies his unwavering loyalty and commitment.

With an unparalleled blend of coaching prowess, passionate demeanor, and a relentless drive for excellence, Jeff Howell stands as a formidable force, shaping not only exceptional athletes but also well-rounded individuals prepared to conquer life's challenges.

Free Bonus:
Program Temperature Guide

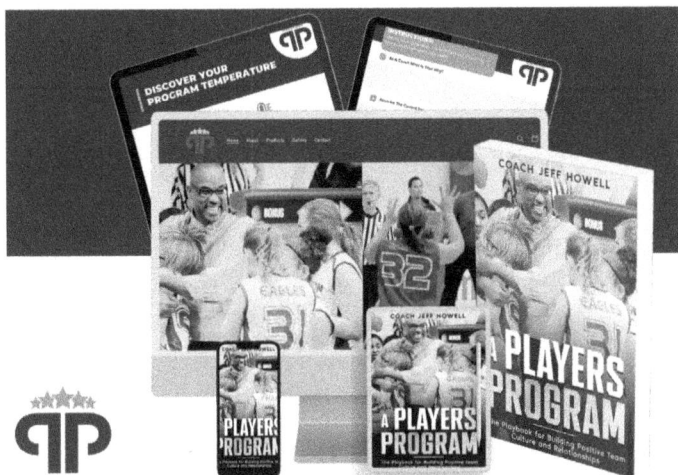

Unlock the secrets to a winning team culture with our exclusive "Program Temperature" guide. Whether you're leading a sports team or any group, this tool helps you gauge and improve your team's dynamics.

Get Your Free Guide!

   1. Assess Your Team: Understand strengths and areas for improvement.

2. **Actionable Steps**: Develop a plan to enhance your team's culture.
3. **Universal Application**: Perfect for coaches, leaders, and educators.

Sign up with your email to get your free "Program Temperature" guide and start transforming your team today!

https://bit.ly/programtemperature

Printed in the USA
CPSIA information can be obtained
at www.ICGtesting.com
CBHW020236080824
12786CB00002B/329